United States
Department of
Agriculture

Forest Service

Northern
Research Station

Resource Bulletin
NRS-63

Indiana Timber Industry: An Assessment of Timber Product Output and Use

2008

Brian F. Walters
Jeff Settle
Ronald J. Piva

Abstract

In 2008, there were 184 primary wood-processing mills in Indiana, 52 fewer mills than in 2005. These mills processed 68.4 million cubic feet of industrial roundwood, of which 58 million cubic feet was harvested from within the State. Another 5.8 million cubic feet of the industrial roundwood harvested in Indiana was sent to primary wood-processing mills in other states and countries. Saw logs accounted for 89 percent of the total harvest. The harvesting of industrial roundwood products produced 50.6 million cubic feet of harvest residues. Primary wood-processing mills generated 1.03 million green tons of mill residues, with less than 1 percent of the mill residues generated not used for other products.

Cover Photo

Young regenerating hardwood forest. Photo used with permission of Indiana Department of Natural Resources.

Contents

INTRODUCTION

Indiana's wood products manufacturing industry[1] employs almost 30,000 workers and has an output of more than $7 billion (U.S. Census Bureau 2007). Given the importance of this industry to the economy of Indiana, this bulletin analyzes recent forest industry trends and reports the results of a detailed study of forest industry, industrial roundwood production, and associated primary mill wood and bark residue in 2008. Such detailed information is necessary for intelligent planning and decisionmaking in wood procurement, economic research, forest resources management, and forest industry development.

The last published report of timber product output and use in Indiana (Piva and Gallion 2007) covered a 2005 study and is used here for comparison. When new surveys are completed, errors and omissions from previous surveys are corrected. As a result of our ongoing efforts to improve the survey's efficiency and reliability, changes may have been made to the previous survey's data. All comparisons and analysis in this report are based on the reprocessed data from earlier surveys, which may not match earlier published data. Rows and columns of supporting tables may not sum due to rounding, but data in each table cell are accurately displayed.

Information about the forest resources of Indiana is available at the Forest Inventory and Analysis Web site at: http://nrs.fs.fed.us/fia/data-tools/state-reports/IN.

The Authors

BRIAN F. WALTERS is a forester with the Forest Inventory and Analysis (FIA) program at the Northern Research Station in St. Paul, MN. He received a B.S. in forestry in 2005 and an M.S. in geographic information science in 2008 from Michigan State University.

JEFF SETTLE is a forest products specialist. He has 25 years of experience with the Indiana Division of Forestry with the last 16 years in the Forest Product Utilization & Marketing program.

RONALD J. PIVA is a forester with the FIA program at the Northern Research Station in St. Paul, MN. He received a B.S. in forest management from the University of Missouri-Columbia in 1984 and joined the Forest Service in 1987.

---

[1] North American Industry Classification System (NAICS) 321 - wood product manufacturing and NAICS 322 - paper manufacturing.

STUDY METHODS

This study was a cooperative effort between the Indiana Department of Natural Resources (IN DNR) Division of Forestry and the Forest Inventory and Analysis (FIA) unit at the Northern Research Station (NRS) of the U.S. Forest Service. The FIA program is responsible for providing forest resource statistics for all ownerships across the United States, including timber product outputs.

IN DNR Division of Forestry personnel surveyed all known primary wood-using mills, using questionnaires supplied by NRS, to obtain a 100-percent response rate. The questionnaires were designed to determine the size and composition of the State's primary wood-using industry, its use of roundwood, and its generation and disposition of wood residues. Completed questionnaires were sent to NRS for processing and analysis. As part of data processing, all industrial roundwood volumes reported on the questionnaires were converted to standard units of measure using regional conversion factors (Table 1). Timber removals by source of material and harvest residues generated during logging were estimated from standard product volumes using factors developed from logging utilization studies previously conducted by NRS. To provide a complete assessment of Indiana's timber product output, data on the State's industrial roundwood receipts were loaded into a regional timber removals database where they were supplemented with data on out-of-State uses of Indiana roundwood.

Certain terms used in this report—retained, exports, imports, production, and receipts— have specialized meanings and relationships unique to the FIA program that surveys timber product output (TPO) (Fig. 1). Tables in this bulletin about saw log and veneer log volumes and sawtimber removal volumes are presented in both International ¼-inch rule and Doyle rule. International ¼-inch rule is the U.S. Forest Service standard; Doyle rule is the common measure used in Indiana by forest industries and land management agencies.

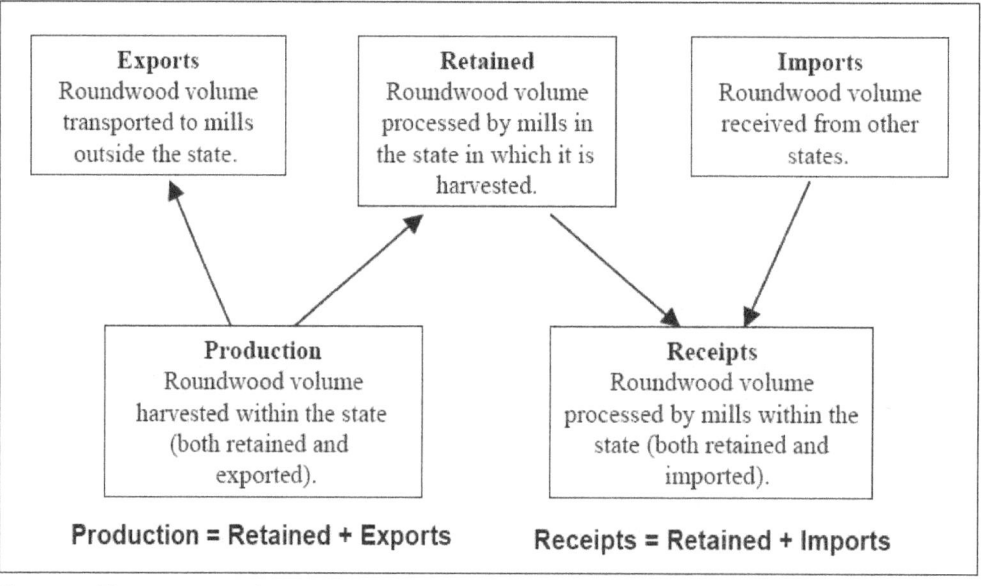

Figure 1.—The movement of industrial roundwood.

Table 1.—Conversion factors from reported unit of measure to standard unit of measure[a]

Product (Standard unit of measure)	Reported unit of measure					
	International ¼-inch rule MBF	Doyle rule MBF	Green tons	Standard cords	Thousand pieces	Thousand cubic feet
Saw logs and handles MBF International ¼-inch rule (MBF Doyle rule)	1 (0.72464)	1.38 (1)	0.2174 (0.15754)	0.5 (0.36232)	--	0.158 (0.114493)
Veneer logs and cooperage MBF International ¼-inch rule (MBF Doyle rule)	1 (0.87719)	1.14 (1)	0.2174 (0.1907)	0.5 (0.4386)	--	0.158 (0.1386)
Pulp and composite products, and industrial fuelwood (Standard cords)	--	--	0.4167	1	--	0.085
Mine timbers (Thousand cubic feet)	--	0.2322	--	0.079	6.7	1
Poles (Pieces)	20	--	4.348	10	1,000	0.0079
Posts (Thousand pieces)	0.2	--	0.04167	0.1	1	0.79
Cabin logs, excelsior/shavings, and miscellaneous products (Thousand cubic feet)	0.158	0.21804	0.0329193	0.079	7.9	1

[a]Reported volume times conversion factor = standard volume. For example, a sawmill reports receiving 100 MBF Doyle rule of roundwood; to convert that to MBF International ¼-inch rule: 100 * 1.38 = 138 MBF.

PRIMARY TIMBER INDUSTRY IN INDIANA
Industrial Roundwood

- Indiana's primary wood-using industry included 155 sawmills, 8 veneer mills, and 21 mills that produced other products (Table 2, Fig. 2).

- Sawmills in the State decreased from 212 in 2005 to 155 in 2008 with most of the decrease occurring among the small mills. Indiana also had a decrease in the number of veneer mills; however, there was an increase in the number of mills producing other wood products.

- Receipts of industrial roundwood at Indiana primary wood-using mills totaled 68.4 million cubic feet in 2008, a decrease of 19 percent from the 84.2 million cubic feet received in 2005 (Table 3).

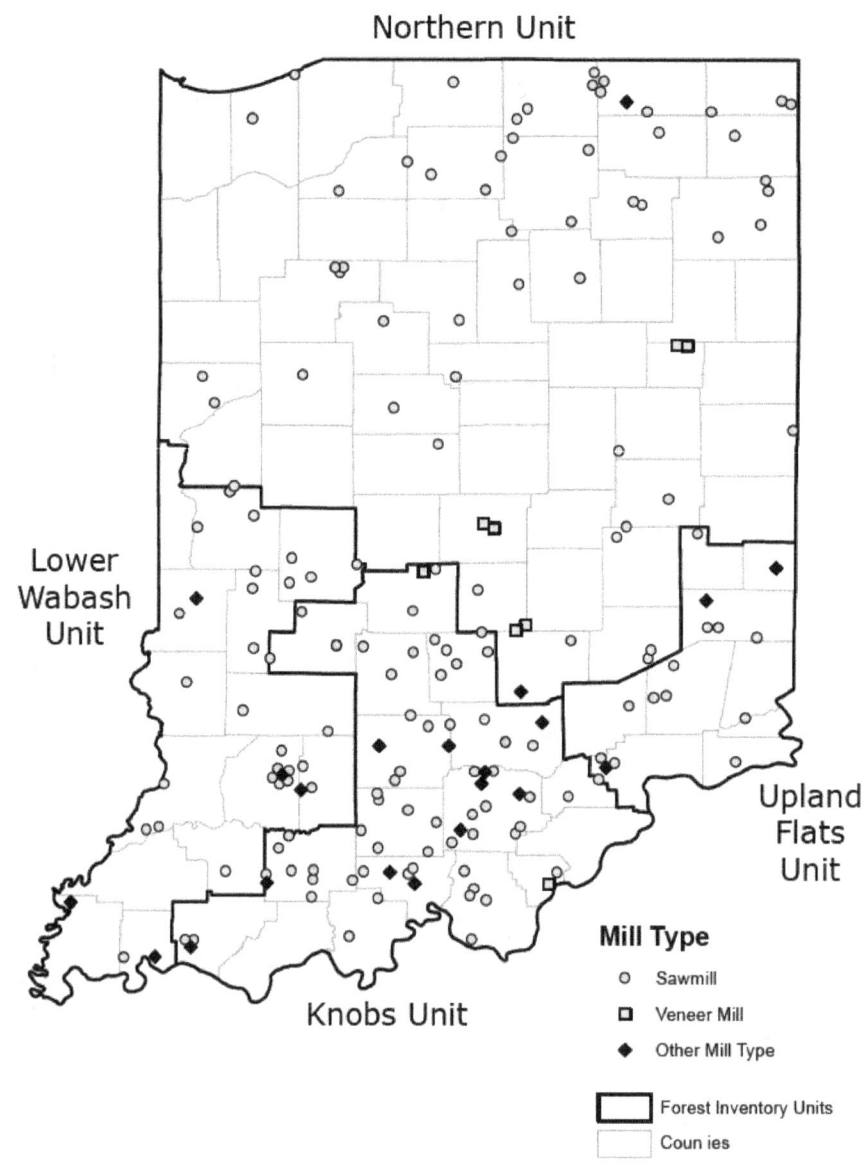

Figure 2.—Indiana Forest Inventory Units and approximate locations of primary wood-using mills, 2008.

- Nearly 85 percent of the industrial roundwood processed by Indiana's primary wood-using mills was harvested from forests within the State. Michigan, Kentucky, Illinois, and Ohio collectively supplied 13 percent of the industrial roundwood consumed by Indiana mills (Table 4).

- Ninety-eight percent of the industrial roundwood processed by Indiana primary wood-using mills was made up of hardwoods. White oaks, red oaks, and yellow-poplar combined accounted for more than 50 percent of the total volume processed. Softwoods accounted for 2 percent of the volume processed and were composed mainly of pine species.

- Industrial roundwood production decreased by 14 percent, from 74.2 million cubic feet in 2005 to 63.8 million cubic feet in 2008 (Table 5, Fig. 3).

- Ninety-one percent of industrial roundwood harvested in Indiana was retained for processing by primary wood-using mills in the State. Mills in Kentucky, Missouri, and Ohio received more than 80 percent of Indiana industrial roundwood exports (Table 6).

- The Knobs Forest Inventory Unit produced 32 million cubic feet of industrial roundwood, 50 percent of total State production, the most of the Forest Inventory Units. This was followed by the Lower Wabash unit (14.3 million cubic feet, 22 percent of total), the Northern unit (13 million cubic feet, 20 percent of total), and the Upland Flats unit (4.5 million cubic feet, 7 percent of total).

- Production remained steady in the Knobs unit with only a slight increase of 0.2 percent from 2005 to 2008. Industrial roundwood production decreased by 19 percent in the Lower Wabash unit, by 30 percent in the Northern unit, and by 25 percent in the Upland Flats unit (Fig. 4).

- Nineteen percent of the industrial roundwood production volume was from the red oak species group. Yellow-poplar (17 percent), white oaks (17 percent), hard maple (8 percent), hickory (7 percent), and ash (7 percent) were other major species groups harvested (Table 7, Fig. 5).

- The production of saw logs accounted for 89 percent of total industrial roundwood production. Pulp and composite products and veneer logs were second in production, each accounting for slightly less than 4 percent of the total volume (Table 8, Fig. 6).

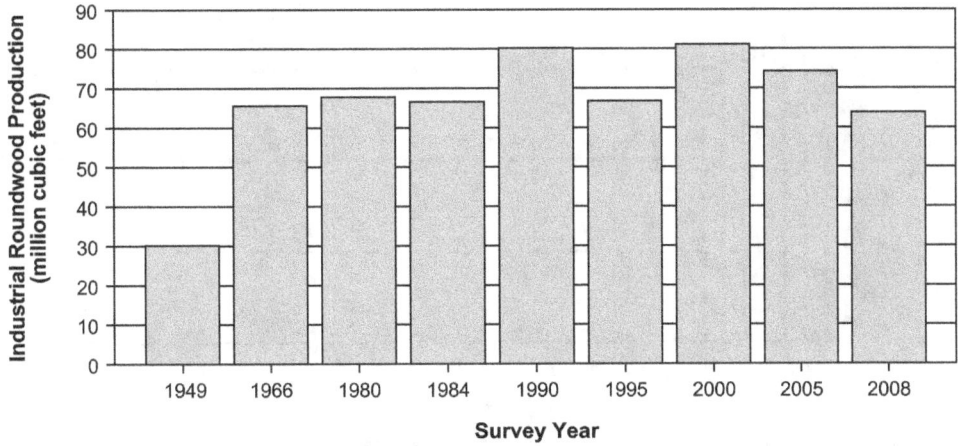

Figure 3.—Industrial roundwood production by survey year, Indiana (Hutchison 1956; Spencer 1969; Blyth et al. 1982, 1987; Hackett and Mayer 1993; Hackett and Settle 1998; Piva and Gallion 2003, 2007).

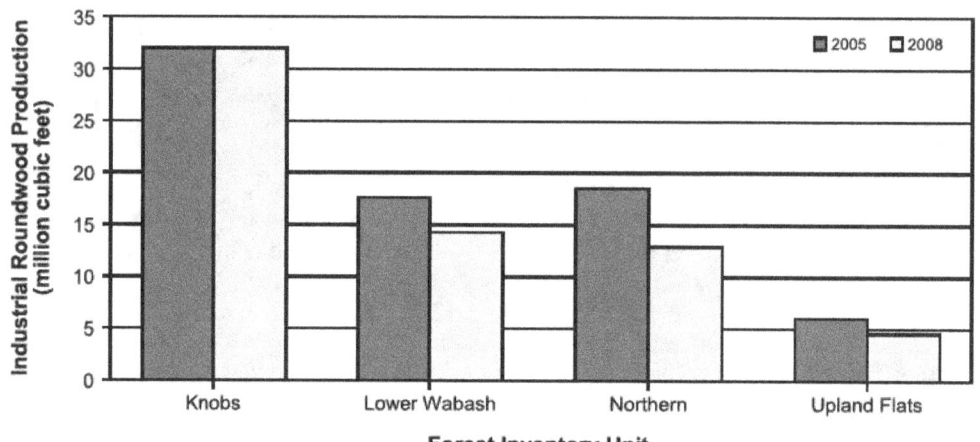

Figure 4.—Industrial roundwood production by Forest Inventory Unit, Indiana, 2005 and 2008 (Piva and Gallion 2007).

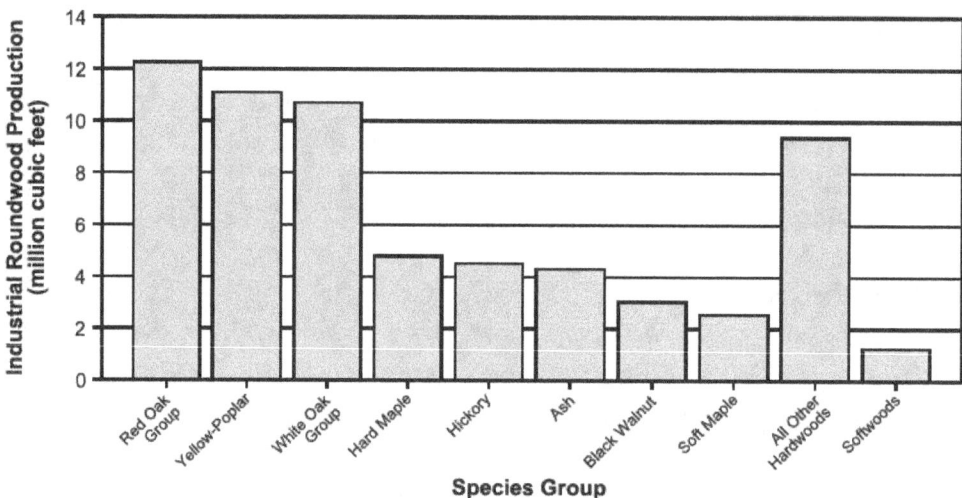

Figure 5.—Industrial roundwood production by species group, Indiana, 2008.

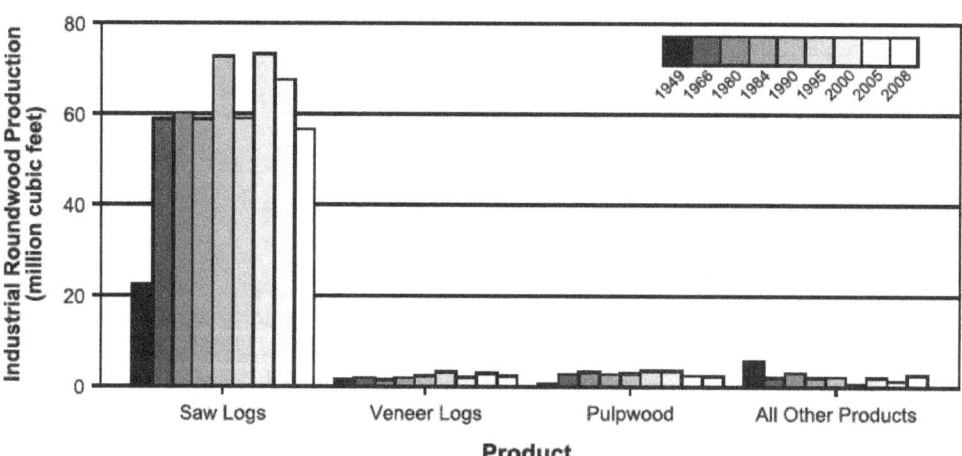

Figure 6.—Industrial roundwood production by product and survey year, Indiana (Hutchison 1956; Spencer 1969; Blyth et al. 1982, 1987; Hackett and Mayer 1993; Hackett and Settle 1998; Piva and Gallion 2003, 2007).

Saw Logs

The International ¼-inch rule is the U.S. Forest Service standard unit of measure for volume of saw and veneer logs. However, the Doyle rule is a widely applied unit of measure in Indiana. Therefore, saw and veneer log volumes will first be presented here using the International ¼-inch rule and the Doyle rule volume will follow in parentheses.

- Receipts at Indiana sawmills totaled 376.6 million board feet (272.9 million board feet Doyle) in 2008, a decrease of 17 percent from 454.2 million board feet (329.2 million board feet Doyle) in 2005 (Tables 9a and 9b).

- Saw log production decreased by 16 percent between 2005 and 2008, from 406.8 million board feet (294.8 million board feet Doyle) to 341.0 million board feet (247.1 million board feet Doyle).

- The red oak species group accounted for nearly 20 percent of the total volume of saw logs produced in Indiana. Other important species groups in saw log production were yellow-poplar (19 percent of total), white oaks (14 percent of total), and hard maple and hickory (7.5 percent of total each) (Fig. 7).

Other Products

- Indiana veneer mill receipts totaled 21.9 million board feet (19.2 million board feet Doyle). A majority of the industrial roundwood used in Indiana veneer mills was imported, with only 41 percent harvested from within the State.

- Production of veneer logs from Indiana forests totaled 16.7 million board feet (14.6 million board feet Doyle) (Table 8).

- Despite the State not having a pulp or composite product mill in 2008, Indiana pulpwood production amounted to 2.3 million cubic feet (29.5 thousand cords), a decrease of 4 percent from 2005 (Table 5).

- Production of industrial roundwood for other products, such as cooperage, handles, cabin logs, and excelsior, was 2.6 million cubic feet, an increase of nearly 100 percent from 2005.

- Residential fuelwood is not included in this report.

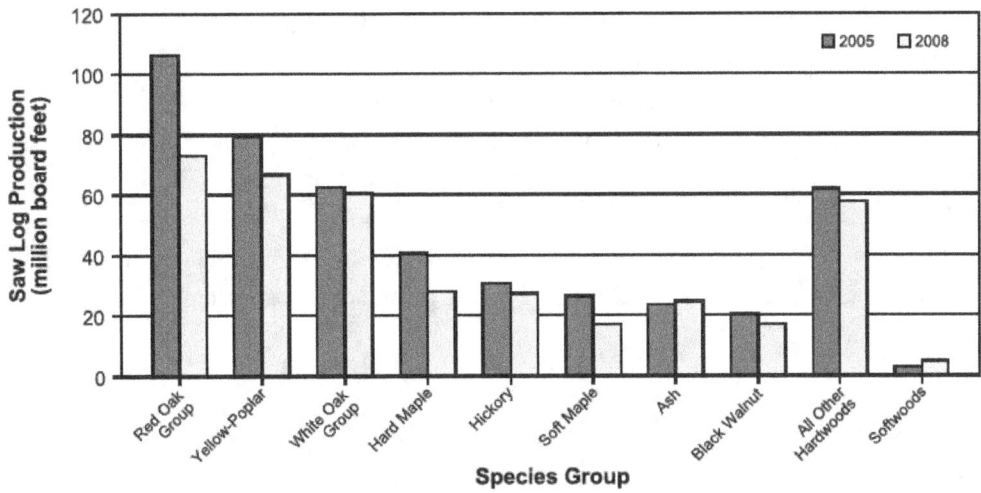

Figure 7.—Saw log production by species group, Indiana, 2005 and 2008 (Piva and Gallion 2007).

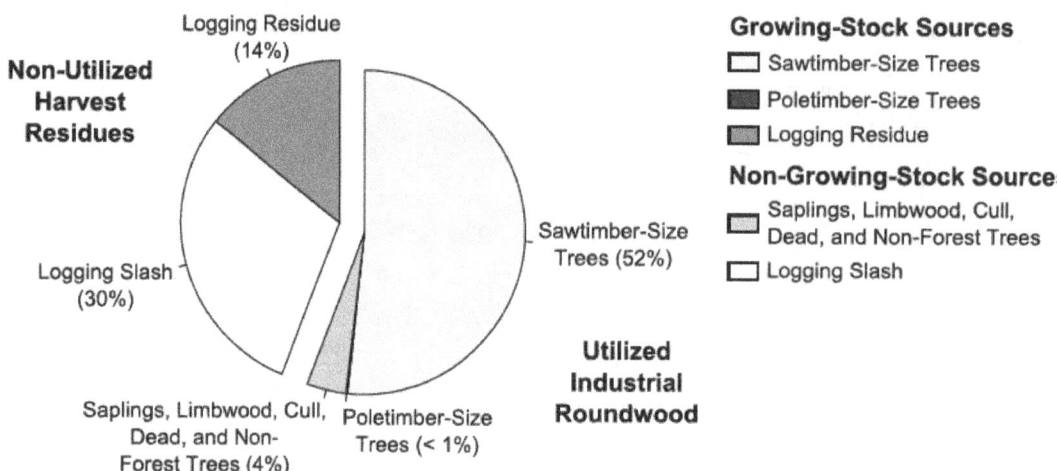

Figure 8.—Distribution of timber removals for industrial roundwood by source of material, Indiana, 2008.

Timber Removals

- During the harvest of industrial roundwood from Indiana's forests in 2008, 114.5 million cubic feet of wood material was cut with 63.8 million cubic feet (56 percent) used for primary wood products (Table 10, Fig. 8).

- Growing-stock sources, at 75.7 million cubic feet, were the largest component of removals for industrial roundwood production. Seventy-eight percent of the growing stock removed was used for products and 22 percent was left as logging residue. Sawtimber-size trees accounted for more than 99 percent of the growing-stock volume used for products.

- Non-growing-stock sources of industrial roundwood production amounted to 38.8 million cubic feet of wood material removed. Only 12 percent of this material was used for products; the remainder was left on the ground as logging slash. Fifty-seven percent of the non-growing-stock material used for industrial roundwood came from the limbs of growing-stock trees; the remainder was made up of cull, dead, and nonforest trees.

- Fifty-one percent of the total growing-stock material removed from Indiana's timberland came from the Knobs Forest Inventory Unit, followed by the Lower Wabash unit with 21 percent, the Northern unit with 20 percent, and the Upland Flats unit with 7 percent (Table 11).

- More than 403.3 million board feet (292.3 million board feet Doyle) was removed from Indiana's sawtimber inventory. Red oaks, yellow-poplar, white oaks, hard maple, hickory, and ash accounted for 75 percent of the total sawtimber volume removed (Tables 12a and 12b).

- The harvest of industrial roundwood from Indiana's forests left 50.6 million cubic feet (1.6 million green tons) of wood material on the ground as harvest residues (Table 13).

Harvest Intensity

- Statewide, there was 66 cubic feet of annual net growth (gross growth minus mortality) of growing stock per acre of forest land and 24 cubic feet of harvest-related wood removals per acre of forest land, a net growth to removal ratio of 2.75.

- The average harvest intensity among Indiana counties was 21.6 cubic feet of wood removals per acre of forest land (Fig. 9).

- In 2008, there were 4.7 million acres of forest land in Indiana (Woodall et al. 2009). The net volume in live trees on forest land was 9.8 billion cubic feet. The 114.5 million cubic feet of total wood material removed due to harvesting (Table 10) was 1.2 percent of the total live volume of trees.

- The Knobs unit had the greatest harvest intensity, with 32 cubic feet of wood removals per acre of forest land, followed by the Lower Wabash unit with 27 cubic feet of removals per forest land acre, the Northern unit (16 cubic feet/acre), and the Upland Flats unit (15 cubic feet/acre).

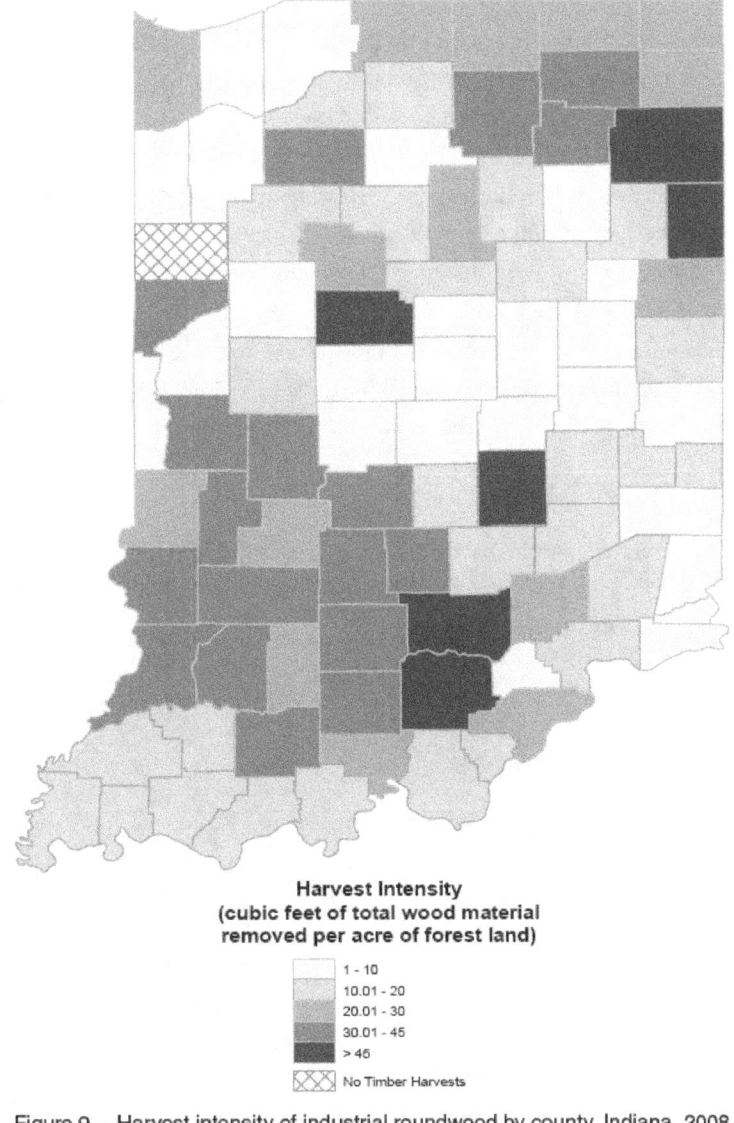

**Harvest Intensity
(cubic feet of total wood material
removed per acre of forest land)**

- 1 - 10
- 10.01 - 20
- 20.01 - 30
- 30.01 - 45
- > 45
- No Timber Harvests

Figure 9.—Harvest intensity of industrial roundwood by county, Indiana, 2008.

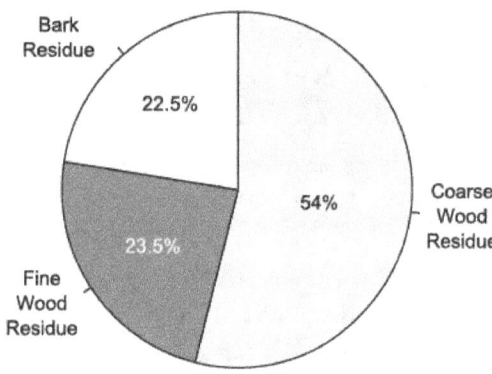

Figure 10.—Residues generated by primary wood-using mills by type of residue generated, Indiana, 2008.

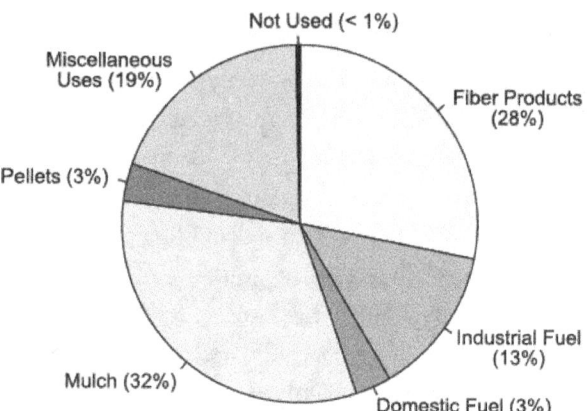

Figure 11.—Disposal of mill residue by product, Indiana, 2008.

Primary Mill Residues

- In converting industrial roundwood into products, Indiana's primary wood-using industries generated a combined 1.0 million green tons of coarse wood residue (slabs, edgings, and veneer cores), fine wood residue (sawdust and veneer clippings), and bark residue (Table 14, Fig. 10).

- Thirty-two percent of mill residues generated were used to make mulch. Fiber products consumed 28 percent of mill residues and miscellaneous uses, such as livestock bedding and small dimension lumber, consumed 19 percent. Only 0.35 percent of residues generated went unused (Fig. 11).

- The top disposal method of coarse wood residue was fiber products at 49 percent of the total. Miscellaneous uses (59 percent) were the top disposal method for fine wood residue; mulch (89 percent) was the top use for bark residues.

ACKNOWLEDGMENTS

Special thanks are given to the primary wood-using firms for supplying information for this study and to the Indiana Department of Natural Resources Division of Forestry for its cooperation in canvassing survey respondents.

LITERATURE CITED

Blyth, J.E.; McGuire, D.H. 1974. **Indiana saw log production and sawmill industry, 1971**. Resour. Bull. NC-20. St. Paul, MN: U.S. Department of Agriculture, Forest Service, North Central Experiment Station. 23 p.

Blyth, J.E.; McGuire, D.H.; Smith, W.B. 1982. **Primary forest products industry and timber use, Indiana, 1980**. Resour. Bull. NC-65. St. Paul, MN: U.S. Department of Agriculture, Forest Service, North Central Forest Experiment Station. 25 p.

Blyth, J.E.; McGuire, D.H.; Smith, W.B. 1987. **Indiana timber industry – an assessment of timber product output and use**. Resour. Bull. NC-102. St. Paul, MN: U.S. Department of Agriculture, Forest Service, North Central Experiment Station. 34 p.

Hackett, R.L.; Mayer, R.W. 1993. **Indiana timber industry – an assessment of timber product output and use, 1990**. Resour. Bull. NC-146. St. Paul, MN: U.S. Department of Agriculture, Forest Service, North Central Forest Experiment Station. 35 p.

Hackett, R.L.; Settle, J. 1998. **Indiana's timber industry – an assessment of timber product output and use, 1995**. Resour. Bull. NC-193. St. Paul, MN: U.S. Department of Agriculture, Forest Service, North Central Forest Experiment Station. 76 p.

Hutchison, O.K. 1956. **Indiana's forest resources and industries**. For. Resour. Rep. No. 10. Washington, DC: U.S. Department of Agriculture, Forest Service, Central States Experiment Station. 44 p.

Piva, R.J.; Gallion, J. 2003. **Indiana timber industry – an assessment of timber product output and use, 2000**. Resour. Bull. NC-216. St. Paul, MN: U.S. Department of Agriculture, Forest Service, North Central Research Station. 109 p.

Piva, R.J.; Gallion, J. 2007. **Indiana timber industry – an assessment of timber product output and use, 2005**. Resour. Bull. NRS-22. Newtown Square, PA: U.S. Department of Agriculture, Forest Service, Northern Research Station. 106 p.

Spencer, J.S., Jr. 1969. **Indiana's timber**. Resour. Bull. NC-7. St. Paul, MN: U.S. Department of Agriculture, Forest Service, North Central Experiment Station. 63 p.

U.S. Census Bureau. 2007. **2007 Economic Census, Indiana – Table 2 Selected Statistics by Economic Sector and Subsector: 2007**. Generated by Brian Walters using American FactFinder; <http://factfinder.census.gov>. [Accessed August 31, 2011].

Woodall, C.W.; Webb, M.N.; Gallion, J. 2009. **Indiana's forest resources, 2008**. Res. Note NRS-36. Newtown Square, PA: U.S. Department of Agriculture, Forest Service, Northern Research Station. 4 p.

APPENDIX

Definition of Terms

Board foot. Unit of measure applied to roundwood. It relates to lumber that is 1 foot long, 1 foot wide, and 1 inch thick (or its equivalent).

Bolt. A short log no more than 8 feet long, to be sawn for lumber, peeled or sliced for veneer, shaved for excelsior, or converted into shingles, cooperage stock, dimension stock, blocks, blanks, or other products.

Central stem. The portion of a tree between a 1-foot stump and the minimum 4.0-inch top diameter outside bark, or point where the central stem breaks into limbs.

Coarse mill residue. Wood residue suitable for chipping such as slabs, edgings, and veneer cores.

Commercial species. Tree species presently or prospectively suitable for industrial wood products. (Note: Excludes species of typically small size, poor form, or inferior quality such as hophornbeam, Osage-orange, and redbud.)

Cull removals. Net volume of rough and rotten trees plus the net volume in sections of the central stem of growing-stock trees that do not meet regional merchantability standards but are harvested for industrial roundwood products.

Diameter at breast height (d.b.h.). The outside bark diameter at 4.5 feet above the forest floor on the uphill side of the tree. For determining breast height, the forest floor includes the duff layer that may be present, but does not include unincorporated woody debris that may rise above the ground line.

Doyle rule. A simple log rule or formula for estimating the board-foot volume of logs based on a 4-inch slabbing allowance to square the log. This rule is used in the Eastern and Southern United States.

Exports. The volume of roundwood utilized by mills outside the state where the timber was harvested.

Fine mill residue. Wood residue not suitable for chipping, such as sawdust and veneer clippings.

Forest land. Land at least 10-percent stocked with trees of any size, or formerly having had such tree cover, and not currently developed for nonforest use. (Note: Stocking is measured by comparing specified standards with basal area and/or number of trees, age or size, and spacing.) The minimum area for classification of forest land is 1 acre. Roadside, streamside, and shelterbelt strips of timber must have a crown width of at least 120 feet to qualify as forest land. Unimproved roads and trails, streams or other bodies of water, or clearings in forest areas shall be classified as forest if less than 120 feet wide.

Growing-stock removals. The growing-stock volume removed from timberland by harvesting industrial roundwood products. (Note: Includes sawtimber removals, poletimber removals, and logging residues.)

Growing-stock tree. A live timberland tree of commercial species that meets specified standards of size, quality, and merchantability. (Note: Excludes rough, rotten, and dead trees.)

Growing-stock volume. Net volume of growing-stock trees 5.0 inches d.b.h. and larger, from 1 foot above the ground to a minimum 4.0-inch top diameter outside bark of the central stem or to the point where the central stem breaks into limbs.

Hardwoods. Dicotyledonous trees, usually broad-leaved and deciduous.

Harvest residues. The total net volume of unused portions of trees cut or killed by logging. (Note: Includes both logging residues and logging slash.)

Industrial fuelwood. A roundwood product, with or without bark, used to generate energy at manufacturing facilities and schools, correctional institutions, or electric generating plants.

Imports. The volume of roundwood delivered to a mill or group of mills in a specific state but harvested outside that state.

Industrial roundwood exports. The quantity of industrial roundwood harvested in a geographical area and transported to other geographical areas.

Industrial roundwood imports. The quantity of industrial roundwood received from other geographical areas.

Industrial roundwood products. Saw logs, pulpwood, veneer logs, poles, commercial posts, pilings, cooperage logs, particleboard bolts, shaving bolts, lath bolts, charcoal bolts, and chips from roundwood used for pulp or board products.

Industrial roundwood production. The quantity of industrial roundwood harvested in a geographic area plus all industrial roundwood exported to other geographical areas.

Industrial roundwood receipts. The quantity of industrial roundwood received by commercial mills in a geographic area plus all industrial roundwood imported from other geographical areas.

Industrial roundwood retained. The quantity of industrial roundwood harvested from and processed by commercial mills within the same geographical area.

International 1/4-inch rule. A log rule or formula for estimating the board-foot volume of logs, allowing ½ inch of taper for each 4-foot length and assuming ¼ inch of kerf. This rule is used as the U.S. Forest Service standard log rule in the Eastern United States.

Limbwood removals. Net volume of all portions of a tree other than the central stem (including forks, large limbs, tops, and stumps) harvested for industrial roundwood products.

Logging residue. The net volume of unused portions of the merchantable central stem of growing-stock trees cut or killed by logging.

Logging slash. The net volume of unused portions of the unmerchantable (non-growing-stock) sections of trees cut or killed by logging.

Merchantable sections. Refers to sections of the central stem of growing-stock trees that meet either pulpwood or saw log specifications.

Net volume. Gross volume less deductions for rot, sweep, or other defects affecting use for roundwood products.

Noncommercial species. Trees species of typically small size, poor form, or inferior quality that normally do not develop into trees suitable for industrial roundwood products. Noncommercial species are listed in the volume tables as rough trees.

Nonforest land. Land that has never supported forests, and land formerly forested where use for timber management is precluded by development for other uses. (Note: Includes areas used for crops, active Christmas tree plantations, orchards, nurseries, improved pasture, residential areas, city parks, improved roads of any width and adjoining clearings, powerline clearings of any width, and 1- to 39.9-acre areas of water classified by the Bureau of the Census as land.) If intermingled in forest areas, unimproved roads and nonforest strips must be more than 120 feet wide and more than 1 acre to qualify as nonforest land.

Nonforest land removals. Net volume of trees on nonforest lands harvested for industrial roundwood products.

Poletimber. A growing-stock tree at least 5.0 inches d.b.h. but smaller than sawtimber size (9.0 inches d.b.h. for softwoods, 11.0 inches d.b.h. for hardwoods).

Poletimber removals. Net volume in the merchantable central stem of poletimber trees harvested for industrial roundwood products.

Primary wood-using mills. Mills receiving roundwood or chips from roundwood for processing into products such as lumber, veneer, and pulp.

Primary wood-using mill residue. Wood materials (coarse and fine) and bark generated at manufacturing plants that process industrial roundwood into principal products. These residues include wood products obtained incidental to production of principal products and wood materials not utilized for some product.

Production. The quantity of roundwood material harvested in a geographic area plus all roundwood material exported to other geographical areas.

Receipts. The quantity of roundwood material received by commercial mills in a geographic area plus all roundwood material imported from other geographical areas.

Retained. Roundwood volume harvested from and processed by mills within the same state.

Rotten tree. A tree that does not meet regional merchantability standards because of excessive unsound cull.

Rough tree. A tree that does not meet regional merchantability standards because of excessive sound cull (includes forks, sweep and crook, and large branches or knots), including noncommercial tree species.

Roundwood. Logs, bolts, or other round sections cut from trees (including chips from roundwood).

Sapling. A live tree between 1.0 and 5.0 inches d.b.h.

Saw log portion. That portion of the central stem of sawtimber trees between the stump and the saw log top.

Saw log top. The point on the central stem of sawtimber trees above which a saw log cannot be produced. The minimum saw log top is 7.0 inches diameter outside bark for softwoods and 9.0 inches diameter outside bark for hardwoods.

Sawtimber removals. As used in Table 10, sawtimber removals refers to the net volume in the merchantable central stem of sawtimber-size trees harvested for industrial roundwood products. (Note: includes the saw log and upper stem portions of sawtimber-size trees.) When referring to the sawtimber volume removed from timberland as in Table 12, sawtimber removals refers to the net volume in the saw log portion of sawtimber-size trees harvested for roundwood products or left on the ground as harvest residue, and is usually expressed in thousands of board feet (International ¼-inch rule).

Sawtimber tree. A growing-stock tree containing at least a 12-foot saw log or two noncontiguous saw logs 8 feet or longer, and meeting regional specifications for freedom from defect. Softwoods must be at least 9.0 inches d.b.h. and hardwoods must be at least 11.0 inches d.b.h.

Sawtimber volume. Net volume in the saw log portion of sawtimber trees.

Softwoods. Coniferous trees, usually evergreen, having needles or scale-like leaves.

Timber product output. The volume of roundwood products produced from an area's forests.

Timberland. Forest land that is producing, or is capable of producing, in excess of 20 cubic feet per acre per year of industrial roundwood products under natural conditions, is not withdrawn from timber utilization by statute or administrative regulation, and is not associated with urban or rural development.

Tree. A woody perennial plant, typically large, with a single well-defined stem carrying a more or less definite crown; sometimes defined as attaining a minimum diameter of 3 in. (7.6 cm) and a minimum height of 15 ft (4.6 m) at maturity. For FIA, any plant on the tree list in the current field manual is measured as a tree.

Upper stem portion. That portion of the central stem of sawtimber trees between the saw log top and the minimum top diameter of 4.0 inches outside bark, or to the point where the central stem breaks into limbs.

Common and Scientific Names of Tree Species by Species Group

Softwoods

Cedars

Atlantic white-cedar	*Chamaecyparis thyoides*
Eastern redcedar	*Juniperus virginiana*
Balsam fir	*Abies balsamea*
Eastern hemlock	*Tsuga canadensis*
Shortleaf pine	*Pinus echinata*
Loblolly pine	*Pinus taeda*
Red pine	*Pinus resinosa*
White pine	*Pinus strobes*

Other pines

Table Mountain pine	*Pinus pungens*
Pitch pine	*Pinus rigida*
Scotch pine	*Pinus sylvestris*
Virginia pine	*Pinus virginiana*

Spruce

Norway spruce	*Picea abies*
White spruce	*Picea glauca*
Red spruce	*Picea rubens*

Hardwoods

Ash

White ash	*Fraxinus americana*
Black ash	*Fraxinus nigra*
Green ash	*Fraxinus pennsylvanica*

Aspen/balsam poplar

Bigtooth aspen	*Populus grandidentata*
Quaking aspen	*Populus tremuloides*

Basswood

American basswood	*Tilia americana*
White basswood	*Tilia heterophylla*
American beech	*Fagus grandifolia*
Yellow birch	*Betula alleghaniensis*
Paper birch	*Betula papyifera*

Other birch

Sweet birch	*Betula lenta*
River birch	*Betula nigra*
Black cherry	*Prunus serotina*
Black walnut	*Juglans nigra*

Elm

Winged elm	*Ulmus alata*
American elm	*Ulmus americana*
Slippery elm	*Ulmus rubra*

Hickory
  Mockernut hickory   *Carya alba*
  Bitternut hickory   *Carya cordiformis*
  Pignut hickory   *Carya glabra*
  Shellbark hickory   *Carya laciniosa*
  Shagbark hickory   *Carya ovata*
Hard maple
  Black maple   *Acer nigrum*
  Sugar maple   *Acer saccharum*
Soft maple
  Boxelder   *Acer negundo*
  Striped maple   *Acer pensylvanicum*
  Red maple   *Acer rubrum*
  Silver maple   *Acer saccharinum*
  Mountain maple   *Acer spicatum*
Red oak group
  Scarlet oak   *Quercus coccinea*
  Southern red oak   *Quercus falcata*
  Shingle oak   *Quercus imbricaria*
  Pin oak   *Quercus palustris*
  Northern red oak   *Quercus rubra*
  Black oak   *Quercus velutina*
White oak group
  White oak   *Quercus alba*
  Swamp white oak   *Quercus bicolor*
  Swamp chestnut oak   *Quercus michauxii*
  Chinkapin oak   *Quercus muehlenbergii*
  Chestnut oak   *Quercus prinus*
  Post oak   *Quercus stellata*
Sweetgum   *Liquidambar styraciflua*
American sycamore   *Platanus occidentalis*
Yellow-poplar   *Liriodendron tulipifera*
Other hardwoods
  Ohio buckeye   *Aesculus glabra*
  Yellow buckeye   *Aeseulus octandra*
  Common serviceberry   *Amelanchier arborea*
  American hornbeam   *Carpinus caroliniana*
  American chestnut   *Castanea dentata*
  Northern catalpa   *Catalpa speciosa*
  Hackberry   *Celtis occidentalis*
  Eastern redbud   *Cercis canadensis*
  Flowering dogwood   *Cornus florida*
  Hawthorn spp.   *Crataegus spp.*
  Common persimmon   *Diospyros virginiana*
  Honeylocust   *Gleditsia triacanthos*
  Butternut   *Juglans cinerea*

Cucumbertree	*Magnolia acuminata*
Mountain or Fraser magnolia	*Magnolia fraseri*
Umbrella magnolia	*Magnolia tripetala*
Apple spp.	*Malus spp.*
Blackgum	*Nyssa sylvatica*
Eastern hophornbeam	*Ostrya virginiana*
Sourwood	*Oxydendrum arboreum*
Paulownia, empress-tree	*Paulownia tomentosa*
Pin cherry	*Prunus pensylvanica*
Chokecherry	*Prunus virginiana*
Black locust	*Robinia pseudoacacia*
Black willow	*Salix nigra*
Sassafras	*Sassafras albidum*
American mountain-ash	*Sorbus americana*

Tables

Table 2.—Number of active primary wood-using mills by mill type and survey year, Indiana[a]

Mill type	Survey year									
	1961	1966	1971	1980[b]	1984	1990[b]	1995	2000	2005	2008
Sawmills										
Large[c]	NA	86	77	99	112	125	107	110	93	79
Medium[d]	NA	55	52	59	47	27	19	16	20	16
Small[e]	NA	339	256	176	117	91	64	58	99	60
Total	400	480	385	334	276	243	190	184	212	155
Veneer mills	19	21	18	16	16	15	11	12	13	8
Pulp and particleboard mills	3	3	3	3	3	3	3	1	1	0
Other mills[f]	22	15	NA	16	13	10	3	9	10	21
All mills	444	519	406	369	308	271	207	206	236	184

NA Data not available.

[a] Mills that produce more than one product are counted only for the product they process the most of.
[b] Number of active sawmills estimated in 1980 and 1990.
[c] Annual lumber production in excess of 1 million board feet.
[d] Annual lumber production from 1/2 million to 1 million board feet.
[e] Annual lumber production less than 1/2 million board feet.
[f] Includes mills producing handles, cooperage, excelsior, etc.

Table 3.—Industrial roundwood receipts, in million cubic feet, by mill type, survey year, and softwoods and hardwoods, Indiana

Mill type	Survey year							
	1966	1980	1984	1990	1995	2000	2005	2008
All species								
Saw logs	32.8	60.2	58.9	84.4	67.4	81.5	75.5	62.7
Veneer logs	2.2	1.5	1.9	5.3	5.9	5.0	5.4	3.1
Other products[a]	10.4	6.2	4.8	4.8	2.4	4.5	3.2	2.8
Total	45.4	67.8	65.6	94.4	75.7	91.1	84.2	68.4
Softwoods								
Saw logs	0.2	0.1	0.2	0.1	0.2	0.7	0.5	0.9
Veneer logs	--	--	0.0	0.0	0.0	0.0	0.0	0.0
Other products[a]	0.1	0.1	--	0.0	0.0	0.1	0.2	0.4
Total	0.3	0.2	0.2	0.1	0.2	0.8	0.7	1.3
Hardwoods								
Saw logs	32.6	60.1	58.7	84.3	67.2	80.8	75.0	61.9
Veneer logs	2.2	1.5	1.9	5.3	5.8	5.0	5.4	3.0
Other products[a]	10.3	6.0	4.8	4.8	2.4	4.4	3.1	2.1
Total	45.1	67.6	65.4	94.3	75.5	90.3	83.5	67.1

[a] Includes pulp mills, handle plants, cabin log mills, etc. Products that had fewer than three mills are combined to prevent disclosure of an individual mill's receipts.

All table cells without observations are indicated by -- . Table value of 0.0 indicates the volume rounds to less than 1 thousand cubic feet. Columns and rows may not add to their totals due to rounding.

Table 4.—Industrial roundwood receipts, in thousand cubic feet, by species group and state of origin, Indiana, 2008

						State of origin								
Species group	Total	Illinois	Indiana	Iowa	Kentucky	Michigan	Missouri	New York	Ohio	Pennsyl- vania	Tenn- essee	West Virginia	Wis- consin	Other U.S.[a]
Softwoods														
Eastern redcedar	91	--	47	--	44	--	--	--	--	--	--	--	--	--
Loblolly/shortleaf pine	44	--	34	--	3	--	--	--	1	3	1	1	--	--
Red pine	9	--	7	--	--	2	--	--	--	--	--	--	--	--
White pine	653	--	608	--	33	12	--	--	--	--	--	--	--	--
Other pine	477	--	465	--	7	3	--	--	--	--	--	--	--	2
Softwood total	1,273	--	1,160	--	86	17	--	--	1	3	1	1	--	2
Hardwoods														
Ash	4,302	57	3,819	1	62	227	--	--	132	1	0	1	--	--
Aspen/balsam poplar	65	--	44	--	--	21	--	--	--	--	--	--	--	--
Basswood	675	--	595	--	3	51	--	--	24	--	--	0	2	--
Beech	1,008	--	972	--	15	12	--	--	9	--	0	--	--	--
White birch	10	--	2	--	1	--	--	1	0	2	0	1	4	--
Yellow birch	6	--	--	--	--	6	--	--	--	--	--	--	--	--
Black cherry	2,829	51	2,092	4	118	371	3	2	76	70	13	20	10	--
Black walnut	3,120	47	2,426	9	148	144	8	22	129	102	42	38	7	--
Cottonwood	1,452	32	1,386	--	--	27	--	--	7	--	--	--	--	--
Elm	285	10	214	--	4	47	--	--	10	--	--	--	--	--
Hickory	4,579	60	4,186	--	94	143	--	5	71	7	0	13	1	--
Hard maple	5,234	49	4,493	14	194	321	7	27	73	34	3	12	7	--
Soft maple	2,906	56	2,395	--	39	379	--	--	35	--	--	1	2	--
Red oak group	12,812	243	11,182	7	424	564	4	1	250	31	22	77	7	--
White oak group	13,012	198	9,187	61	1,187	567	13	25	1,252	194	48	275	6	--
Sweetgum	495	11	475	--	4	2	--	--	2	--	0	--	--	--
Sycamore	1,453	22	1,397	--	8	23	--	--	3	--	0	--	--	--
Black gum/tupelo	26	--	26	--	--	--	--	--	--	--	--	--	--	--
Yellow-poplar	11,275	183	10,667	--	250	136	0	1	31	3	2	3	--	--
Other hardwoods	1,548	35	1,330	--	32	62	0	2	9	6	2	2	0	66
Hardwood total	67,092	1,053	56,886	97	2,582	3,103	36	86	2,112	450	133	442	46	66
All species	68,365	1,053	58,046	97	2,668	3,120	36	86	2,113	453	135	443	46	68

[a] Includes Texas and Washington.

All table cells without observations are indicated by -- . Table value of 0 indicates the volume rounds to less than 1 thousand cubic feet. Columns and rows may not add to their totals due to rounding.

23

Table 5.—Industrial roundwood production, in thousand cubic feet, by product, softwoods and hardwoods, and survey year, Indiana

Product	Survey year								
	1949	1966	1980	1984	1990	1995	2000	2005	2008
All species									
Saw logs	22,381	58,900	60,159	58,892	72,649	58,998	73,343	67,625	56,630
Veneer logs	1,611	1,900	1,474	1,948	2,307	3,246	2,113	2,875	2,294
Pulpwood	556	2,800	3,179	2,791	2,992	3,509	3,551	2,425	2,337
Cooperage	644	NA	1,344	650	850	301	686	533	1,798
Handles	NA	NA	1,368	1,203	1,108	255	1,215	583	229
Other products[a]	4,991	2,000	293	137	215	137	180	174	551
Total	30,183	65,600	67,817	65,621	80,121	66,446	81,089	74,216	63,839
Softwoods									
Saw logs	56	200	65	155	75	1,013	626	440	836
Veneer logs	--	0	--	3	3	--	--	1	6
Pulpwood	--	--	111	--	--	284	312	296	54
Cooperage	--	--	--	--	--	--	--	--	--
Handles	--	--	--	--	--	--	--	--	--
Other products[a]	94	--	5	--	42	17	76	92	370
Total	150	200	181	158	117	1,315	1,015	829	1,266
Hardwoods									
Saw logs	22,325	58,700	60,094	58,737	72,577	57,984	72,718	67,185	55,794
Veneer logs	1,611	1,900	1,474	1,945	2,304	3,246	2,113	2,874	2,288
Pulpwood	556	2,800	3,068	2,791	2,992	3,509	3,239	2,129	2,283
Cooperage	644	NA	1,344	650	850	301	686	533	1,798
Handles	NA	NA	1,368	1,203	1,108	255	1,215	583	229
Other products[a]	4,897	2,000	288	137	173	120	104	83	181
Total	30,033	65,400	67,636	65,463	80,004	65,415	80,074	73,387	62,573

NA Data not available. Volume is included with other products.

[a] Includes excelsior, shavings, cabin logs, posts, etc.

All table cells without observations are indicated by -- . Table value of 0 indicates the volume rounds to less than 1 thousand cubic feet. Columns and rows may not add to their totals due to rounding.

24

Table 6.—Industrial roundwood production, in thousand cubic feet, by Forest Inventory Unit, species group, and state of destination, Indiana, 2008

ALL UNITS

Species group	Total	Indiana	Kentucky	Michigan	Missouri	North Carolina	Ohio	Tennessee	Virginia	Wisconsin	Canada	Other countries
						State of destination						
Softwoods												
Eastern redcedar	86	47	38	--	--	0	--	--	1	--	--	--
Loblolly/shortleaf pine	40	34	3	--	--	--	3	--	--	--	--	--
Red pine	7	7	--	--	--	--	--	--	--	--	--	--
White pine	640	608	7	--	--	--	25	--	--	--	--	--
Other pine	494	465	3	--	--	--	26	--	--	--	--	--
Softwood total	1,266	1,160	51	--	--	0	54	--	1	--	--	--
Hardwoods												
Ash	4,292	3,819	363	2	--	9	94	--	0	4	0	--
Aspen/balsam poplar	44	44	--	--	--	--	--	--	--	--	--	--
Basswood	620	595	6	0	--	--	20	--	--	15	--	--
Beech	999	972	7	--	--	--	5	--	--	--	--	--
White birch	2	2	--	--	--	--	--	--	--	--	--	--
Other birch	2	--	2	--	--	--	--	--	--	--	--	--
Black cherry	2,346	2,092	70	31	--	135	4	--	7	7	0	--
Black walnut	3,031	2,426	147	126	--	49	206	0	28	2	29	19
Cottonwood	1,437	1,386	50	--	--	--	2	--	--	--	--	--
Elm	256	214	35	--	--	--	3	--	--	--	5	--
Hickory	4,493	4,186	235	1	--	13	9	--	3	46	0	--
Hard maple	4,799	4,493	146	--	--	13	63	--	3	82	1	--
Soft maple	2,549	2,395	120	13	--	--	14	--	--	7	--	--
Red oak group	12,252	11,182	517	11	128	23	279	--	0	48	48	14
White oak group	10,690	9,187	166	41	940	28	230	--	70	--	29	--
Sweetgum	488	475	13	--	--	--	--	--	--	--	--	--
Sycamore	1,637	1,397	227	--	--	--	14	--	--	--	--	--
Tupelo	34	26	7	--	--	1	--	--	--	--	--	--
Yellow-poplar	11,087	10,667	404	--	--	--	16	--	--	--	--	--
Other hardwoods	1,516	1,330	185	1	--	--	--	--	--	--	--	--
Hardwood total	62,573	56,886	2,698	226	1,067	271	957	0	112	210	112	33
State total	63,839	58,046	2,749	226	1,067	271	1,011	0	112	210	112	33

(Table 6 continued on next page)

Table 6.—continued

KNOBS UNIT

Species group	Total	Indiana	Kentucky	Michigan	Missouri	North Carolina	Ohio	Tennessee	Virginia	Wisconsin	Canada	Other countries
Softwoods												
Eastern redcedar	46	38	8	--	--	0	--	--	0	--	0	--
Loblolly/shortleaf pine	35	30	3	--	--	--	3	--	--	--	--	--
Red pine	0	0	--	--	--	--	--	--	--	--	--	--
White pine	402	374	3	--	--	--	25	--	--	--	--	--
Other pine	466	438	2	--	--	--	26	--	--	--	--	--
Softwood total	949	880	15	--	--	0	53	--	0	--	--	--
Hardwoods												
Ash	1,628	1,597	27	--	--	--	--	--	0	4	0	--
Aspen/balsam poplar	32	32	--	--	--	--	--	--	--	--	--	--
Basswood	43	43	--	--	--	--	--	--	--	--	--	--
Beech	609	587	7	--	--	--	--	--	--	15	--	--
White birch	0	0	--	--	--	--	--	--	--	--	--	--
Black cherry	915	866	6	--	--	33	--	--	3	7	0	--
Black walnut	957	909	6	6	--	4	--	0	3	2	19	8
Cottonwood	142	141	0	--	--	--	--	--	--	--	--	--
Elm	49	45	2	--	--	--	--	--	--	--	2	--
Hickory	2,308	2,213	45	--	--	3	--	--	1	46	--	--
Hard maple	2,658	2,525	46	--	--	2	--	--	2	82	1	--
Soft maple	797	749	41	--	--	--	--	--	--	7	--	--
Red oak group	6,549	6,268	105	--	68	3	--	--	0	48	46	10
White oak group	6,691	5,795	99	--	711	6	--	--	53	--	27	--
Sweetgum	152	139	12	--	--	--	--	--	--	--	--	--
Sycamore	583	568	14	--	--	--	--	--	--	--	--	--
Tupelo	21	16	5	--	--	0	--	--	--	--	--	--
Yellow-poplar	6,242	6,124	119	--	--	--	--	--	--	--	--	--
Other hardwoods	701	682	19	--	--	--	--	--	--	--	--	--
Hardwood total	31,076	29,300	555	6	780	50	--	0	61	210	95	18
Unit total	32,025	30,180	571	6	780	51	53	0	62	210	95	18

26

LOWER WABASH UNIT

Species group	Total	Indiana	Kentucky	Michigan	Missouri	North Carolina	Ohio	Tennessee	Virginia	Wisconsin	Canada	Other countries
Softwoods												
Eastern redcedar	1	1	--	--	--	--	--	--	--	--	--	--
Loblolly/shortleaf pine	4	4	0	--	--	--	0	--	--	--	--	--
White pine	160	155	4	--	--	--	0	--	--	--	--	--
Other pine	26	25	1	--	--	--	0	--	--	--	--	--
Softwood total	191	185	5	--	--	--	1	--	--	--	--	--
Hardwoods												
Ash	1,010	676	331	--	--	3	--	--	0	--	0	--
Aspen/balsam poplar	0	0	--	--	--	--	--	--	--	--	--	--
Basswood	51	46	5	--	--	--	--	--	--	--	--	--
Beech	128	128	1	--	--	--	--	--	--	--	--	--
White birch	1	1	--	--	--	--	--	--	--	--	--	--
Other birch	2	--	2	--	--	--	--	--	--	--	--	--
Black cherry	443	368	59	--	--	16	--	--	1	--	1	--
Black walnut	682	503	124	16	--	18	--	0	9	--	5	7
Cottonwood	420	381	39	--	--	--	--	--	--	--	--	--
Elm	54	20	32	--	--	--	--	--	--	--	2	--
Hickory	1,250	1,059	189	--	--	2	--	--	1	--	0	--
Hard maple	939	830	99	--	--	8	--	--	1	--	--	--
Soft maple	739	664	75	--	--	--	--	--	--	--	--	--
Red oak group	2,714	2,251	395	--	60	5	--	--	0	--	--	4
White oak group	1,182	1,030	60	--	77	3	--	--	12	--	--	--
Sweetgum	62	62	0	--	--	--	--	--	--	--	--	--
Sycamore	496	284	212	--	--	--	--	--	--	--	--	--
Tupelo	12	10	3	--	--	--	--	--	--	--	--	--
Yellow-poplar	3,300	3,015	284	--	--	--	--	--	--	--	--	--
Other hardwoods	631	468	163	--	--	--	--	--	--	--	--	--
Hardwood total	14,117	11,796	2,073	16	137	54	--	0	24	--	7	11
Unit total	14,309	11,981	2,078	16	137	54	1	0	24	--	7	11

(Table 6 continued on next page)

27

Table 6.—continued

NORTHERN UNIT

| Species group | Total | State of destination | | | | | | | | | | |
		Indiana	Kentucky	Michigan	Missouri	North Carolina	Ohio	Tennessee	Virginia	Wisconsin	Canada	Other countries
Softwoods												
Red pine	7	7	---	---	---	---	---	---	---	---	---	---
White pine	49	49	---	---	---	---	---	---	---	---	---	---
Softwood total	56	56	---	---	---	---	---	---	---	---	---	---
Hardwoods												
Ash	1,299	1,243	4	2	---	5	45	---	0	---	0	---
Aspen/balsam poplar	11	11	---	---	---	---	---	---	---	---	---	---
Basswood	446	428	0	0	---	---	18	---	---	---	---	---
Beech	166	161	0	---	---	---	5	---	---	---	---	---
Black cherry	824	710	5	31	---	71	3	---	4	---	0	---
Black walnut	1,170	863	12	79	---	17	181	0	10	---	3	4
Cottonwood	861	849	10	---	---	---	1	---	---	---	---	---
Elm	141	137	1	---	---	---	2	---	---	---	1	---
Hickory	635	617	1	1	---	8	7	---	1	---	---	---
Hard maple	973	915	0	---	---	3	54	---	0	---	0	---
Soft maple	844	815	3	13	---	---	14	---	---	---	---	---
Red oak group	2,228	1,991	17	11	---	16	190	---	---	---	2	0
White oak group	2,015	1,798	5	41	---	19	150	---	---	---	1	---
Sweetgum	82	82	---	---	---	---	---	---	---	---	---	---
Sycamore	384	376	0	---	---	---	8	---	---	---	---	---
Tupelo	1	1	---	---	---	1	---	---	---	---	---	---
Yellow-poplar	671	666	0	---	---	---	6	---	---	---	---	---
Other hardwoods	154	150	3	1	---	---	---	---	---	---	---	---
Hardwood total	12,904	11,812	61	180	---	140	684	0	16	---	8	4
Unit total	12,960	11,868	61	180	---	140	684	0	16	---	8	4

UPLAND FLATS UNIT

Species group	Total	Indiana	Kentucky	Michigan	Missouri	North Carolina	Ohio	Tennessee	Virginia	Wisconsin	Canada	Other countries
Softwoods												
Red pine	39	8	31	--	--	0	--	--	0	--	0	--
White pine	29	29	--	--	--	--	--	--	--	--	--	--
Other pine	2	2	--	--	--	--	--	--	--	--	--	--
Softwood total	70	39	31	--	--	0	--	--	0	--	0	--
Hardwoods												
Ash	354	303	1	--	--	1	49	--	0	--	0	--
Basswood	81	79	--	--	--	--	2	--	--	--	--	--
Beech	97	96	--	--	--	--	0	--	--	--	--	--
White birch	0	0	--	--	--	--	--	--	--	--	--	--
Black cherry	165	148	--	--	--	16	1	--	--	--	0	--
Black walnut	222	151	4	24	--	10	25	--	5	--	2	1
Cottonwood	15	15	--	--	--	--	0	--	--	--	--	--
Elm	13	12	--	--	--	--	1	--	--	--	0	--
Hickory	300	297	--	--	--	--	2	--	1	--	--	--
Hard maple	230	221	0	--	--	--	8	--	0	--	--	--
Soft maple	168	168	--	--	--	--	--	--	--	--	--	--
Red oak group	761	672	--	--	--	--	89	--	--	--	--	--
White oak group	802	564	2	--	151	--	80	--	5	--	--	--
Sweetgum	191	191	--	--	--	--	--	--	--	--	--	--
Sycamore	174	168	--	--	--	--	5	--	--	--	--	--
Tupelo	0	0	--	--	--	--	--	--	--	--	--	--
Yellow-poplar	873	862	1	--	--	--	10	--	--	--	--	--
Other hardwoods	31	31	0	--	--	--	--	--	--	--	--	--
Hardwood total	4,475	3,978	9	24	151	27	273	--	11	--	3	1
Unit total	4,545	4,017	39	24	151	27	273	--	11	--	3	1

All table cells without observations are indicated by --. Table value of 0 indicates the volume rounds to less than 1 thousand cubic feet. Columns and rows may not add to their totals due to rounding.

Table 7.—Industrial roundwood production, in thousand cubic feet, by Forest Inventory Unit, county, and species group, Indiana, 2008

Forest Inventory Unit and county	All species	Softwoods						Hardwoods					
		Eastern redcedar	Loblolly/ shortleaf pine	Red pine	White pine	Other pine	Total softwoods	Ash	Aspen/ balsam poplar	Bass-wood	Beech	White birch	Other birch
Knobs Unit													
Brown	3,186	--	2	--	--	--	2	59	0	1	41	0	--
Clark	1,124	2	2	--	0	34	36	127	--	--	46	--	--
Crawford	1,891	3	6	--	--	6	14	33	--	--	4	--	--
Dubois	1,855	--	2	--	5	--	7	131	--	--	15	--	--
Floyd	494	1	--	--	--	9	10	40	--	--	0	--	--
Harrison	1,434	14	--	--	--	81	96	123	7	4	12	--	--
Jackson	2,673	1	--	0	118	80	199	218	6	1	92	0	--
Lawrence	2,762	0	2	--	96	--	99	82	16	--	53	--	--
Monroe	3,456	2	0	--	68	--	70	156	0	18	95	--	--
Morgan	1,542	--	--	--	--	--	--	162	0	10	49	--	--
Orange	2,752	5	5	--	71	15	96	83	2	0	36	--	--
Owen	1,778	0	--	--	--	3	3	107	1	9	48	--	--
Perry	1,516	4	17	--	43	0	64	29	--	9	22	--	--
Scott	514	8	--	--	--	65	73	3	--	14	14	--	--
Spencer	567	0	--	--	--	--	0	56	--	--	12	--	--
Warrick	658	--	2	--	--	--	2	34	--	--	11	--	--
Washington	3,825	5	--	--	--	173	179	186	--	0	59	--	--
Unit total	32,025	46	35	0	402	466	949	1,628	32	43	609	0	--
Lower Wabash Unit													
Clay	995	--	--	--	6	2	9	56	--	--	3	0	--
Daviess	711	--	--	--	--	--	--	36	--	--	0	--	--
Gibson	350	--	--	--	--	--	--	55	--	--	1	--	--
Greene	2,248	--	1	--	17	5	23	22	--	3	16	0	--
Knox	817	--	--	--	--	--	--	161	--	--	1	--	--
Martin	2,239	0	--	--	--	2	2	99	--	1	48	0	0
Parke	1,688	--	--	--	--	--	--	94	--	13	49	--	--
Pike	549	0	4	--	134	16	154	13	--	--	0	1	--
Posey	223	--	--	--	--	--	--	29	--	--	--	--	--
Putnam	1,470	--	--	--	--	--	--	103	--	9	10	--	--
Sullivan	1,989	--	--	--	3	1	4	285	--	1	0	0	2
Vanderburgh	153	--	--	--	--	--	--	13	--	--	--	--	--
Vermillion	192	--	--	--	--	--	--	4	0	4	--	--	--
Vigo	685	--	--	--	--	--	--	41	--	19	--	1	--
Unit total	14,309	1	4	--	160	26	191	1,010	0	51	128	1	2

Forest inventory Unit and county	All species	Eastern redcedar	Loblolly/shortleaf pine	Red pine	White pine	Other pine	Total softwoods	Ash	Aspen/balsam poplar	Bass-wood	Beech	White birch	Other birch
Northern Unit													
Adams	149	--	--	--	--	--	--	4	--	--	--	--	--
Allen	1,379	--	--	--	--	--	--	67	--	295	87	--	--
Bartholomew	337	--	--	--	--	--	--	12	1	--	18	--	--
Blackford	26	--	--	--	--	--	--	4	0	--	1	--	--
Boone	84	--	--	--	--	--	--	28	--	--	--	--	--
Carroll	239	--	--	--	--	--	--	8	--	7	3	--	--
Cass	230	--	--	--	--	--	--	20	--	2	--	--	--
Clinton	65	--	--	--	--	--	--	3	--	--	3	--	--
De Kalb	372	--	--	--	--	--	--	42	--	24	1	--	--
Decatur	367	--	--	--	--	--	--	7	--	--	2	--	--
Delaware	31	--	--	--	--	--	--	1	--	--	--	--	--
Elkhart	550	--	--	5	--	--	5	77	0	7	15	--	--
Fountain	274	--	--	--	--	--	--	16	--	1	0	--	--
Fulton	123	--	--	--	--	--	--	10	0	6	--	--	--
Grant	169	--	--	--	--	--	--	31	0	1	--	--	--
Hamilton	66	--	--	--	--	--	--	17	--	--	--	--	--
Hancock	75	--	--	--	--	--	--	12	--	--	--	--	--
Hendricks	75	--	--	--	--	--	--	11	--	0	--	--	--
Henry	45	--	--	--	--	--	--	1	--	1	--	--	--
Howard	67	--	--	--	--	--	--	10	--	1	--	--	--
Huntington	246	--	--	--	--	--	--	94	0	14	11	--	--
Jasper	99	--	--	--	--	--	--	--	--	--	--	--	--
Jay	207	--	--	--	--	--	--	44	0	2	1	--	--
Johnson	237	--	--	--	--	--	--	69	--	--	7	--	--
Kosciusko	1,031	--	--	--	--	--	--	237	0	14	7	--	--
La Grange	484	--	--	2	12	--	14	28	2	13	0	--	--
La Porte	255	--	--	--	--	--	--	0	0	--	--	--	--
Lake	51	--	--	--	--	--	--	2	0	--	--	--	--
Madison	55	--	--	--	--	--	--	30	--	2	--	--	--
Marion	73	--	--	--	--	--	--	20	--	0	--	--	--
Marshall	428	--	--	--	--	--	--	19	--	7	1	--	--
Miami	287	--	--	--	--	--	--	43	0	5	0	--	--
Montgomery	255	--	--	--	--	--	--	23	2	1	1	--	--
Newton	60	--	--	--	--	--	--	--	--	--	--	--	--
Noble	676	--	--	--	--	--	--	44	--	2	4	--	--
Porter	203	--	--	--	--	--	--	2	0	--	--	--	--
Pulaski	495	--	--	--	--	--	--	--	--	--	--	--	--

(Table 7 continued on the next page)

Table 7.—continued

Randolph	138	--	--	--	--	--	11	--	--	1	--
Rush	89	--	--	--	--	--	24	--	--	--	--
Shelby	102	--	--	--	--	--	15	--	--	--	--
St. Joseph	551	--	--	--	--	--	15	--	4	--	--
Starke	143	--	--	--	--	--	--	--	--	--	--
Steuben	746	--	--	--	--	--	65	1	6	0	0
Tippecanoe	102	--	--	--	--	--	10	--	0	--	--
Tipton	17	--	--	--	--	--	2	--	--	--	--
Wabash	233	0	--	0	0	--	56	--	8	1	--
Warren	169	--	--	--	--	--	5	--	3	--	--
Wayne	39	--	--	--	--	--	3	--	--	--	--
Wells	191	--	--	--	--	--	28	--	0	--	--
White	144	--	--	--	--	--	5	--	4	--	--
Whitley	435	--	37	37	37	--	24	5	15	--	--
Unit total	**12,960**	--	7	49	56	--	1,299	11	446	166	--
Upland Flats Unit											
Dearborn	391	0	--	--	--	--	43	0	2	--	--
Fayette	217	0	--	--	--	--	54	0	--	0	--
Franklin	564	--	--	--	--	--	42	--	--	5	--
Jefferson	811	16	--	2	2	--	35	20	45	3	--
Jennings	1,460	8	--	27	--	--	75	34	14	57	0
Ohio	56	0	--	--	--	--	25	0	--	--	--
Ripley	833	8	--	--	--	--	54	8	19	30	--
Switzerland	106	8	--	--	--	--	13	8	--	--	--
Union	107	0	--	--	--	--	12	0	--	1	--
Unit total	**4,545**	39	--	29	2	--	354	70	81	97	0
State total	**63,839**	86	40	640	494	7	4,292	44	620	999	2

Forest Inventory Unit and county	Hardwoods														
	Black cherry	Black walnut	Cotton-wood	Elm	Hickory	Hard maple	Soft maple	Red oak group	White oak group	Sweet-gum	Syca-more	Tupelo/gum	Yellow-poplar	Other hardwoods	Total hardwoods
Knobs Unit															
Brown	81	38	--	5	272	211	112	1,280	853	0	51	2	131	45	3,185
Clark	14	54	--	0	95	55	17	145	184	25	14	--	304	8	1,088
Crawford	61	22	--	4	207	150	15	474	637	--	49	1	193	26	1,876
Dubois	66	88	--	3	133	141	108	282	419	24	32	3	297	107	1,849
Floyd	8	11	--	--	18	37	7	84	257	0	--	0	11	12	484
Harrison	116	41	1	6	75	196	23	347	164	--	5	1	175	43	1,338
Jackson	67	50	10	2	94	233	127	367	355	42	132	2	644	32	2,473
Lawrence	132	75	4	6	117	179	45	629	322	--	111	1	822	69	2,663
Monroe	130	258	--	5	372	197	61	588	690	5	24	0	722	63	3,385
Morgan	17	44	87	1	105	172	59	329	96	--	18	1	357	33	1,542
Orange	40	94	--	3	120	265	22	668	510	7	43	1	645	115	2,656
Owen	7	23	3	2	125	192	47	214	141	2	6	1	816	30	1,775
Perry	16	16	--	4	163	172	49	315	467	10	9	2	155	23	1,452
Scott	13	29	--	0	24	89	4	6	144	1	1	2	101	9	441
Spencer	38	17	--	0	94	28	48	104	92	19	18	--	7	35	566
Warrick	5	8	36	1	57	22	44	275	72	16	30	1	26	17	657
Washington	105	89	--	6	238	320	12	439	1,286	--	38	1	836	32	3,646
Unit total	915	957	142	49	2,308	2,658	797	6,549	6,691	152	583	21	6,242	701	31,076
Lower Wabash Unit															
Clay	29	40	--	2	40	78	107	343	51	3	31	--	193	10	986
Daviess	14	11	114	2	33	13	89	178	40	6	2	0	142	30	711
Gibson	9	13	29	0	47	16	61	45	5	7	15	--	4	42	350
Greene	83	37	63	2	170	99	164	357	153	2	55	2	922	75	2,225
Knox	0	42	2	5	1	101	20	147	6	1	1	--	279	50	817
Martin	45	24	7	3	285	219	39	386	372	--	30	5	650	25	2,237
Parke	81	141	--	6	97	153	5	234	234	--	55	1	436	91	1,688
P ke	16	4	88	1	18	17	17	91	10	26	21	1	31	40	395
Posey	5	1	--	0	14	3	7	82	36	13	10	1	12	9	223
Putnam	38	159	--	1	228	152	30	156	167	--	1	1	369	45	1,470
Sullivan	75	146	8	25	258	31	58	441	57	--	247	2	184	165	1,986
Vanderburgh	0	--	92	0	1	1	16	11	1	3	1	--	13	14	153
Vermillion	4	5	--	--	17	4	--	104	17	--	0	--	27	7	192
Vigo	42	59	17	6	43	53	127	140	34	--	24	--	38	41	685
Unit total	443	682	420	54	1,250	939	739	2,714	1,182	62	496	12	3,300	631	14,117

(Table 7 continued on the next page)

33

Table 7.—continued

Forest Inventory Unit and county	Black cherry	Black walnut	Cotton- wood	Elm	Hickory	Hard maple	Soft maple	Hardwoods Red oak group	White oak group	Sweet- gum	Syca- more	Tupelo/ gum	Yellow- poplar	Other hardwoods	Total hardwoods
Northern Unit															
Adams	41	10	0	1	14	1	--	25	47	4	1	--	1	0	149
Allen	16	133	0	8	65	146	53	232	263	4	0	--	3	7	1,379
Bartholomew	2	4	--	1	16	26	13	99	17	13	7	--	107	1	337
Blackford	0	9	1	0	1	1	0	4	5	10	--	--	--	--	26
Boone	4	3	--	3	6	3	0	7	17	10	--	--	--	2	84
Carroll	7	21	33	--	14	15	34	42	54	--	--	0	0	--	239
Cass	10	10	--	0	7	28	2	91	56	3	1	--	0	--	230
Clinton	--	1	24	--	3	3	3	3	3	--	6	--	9	2	65
De Kalb	9	37	0	9	9	28	103	25	25	4	50	--	7	0	372
Decatur	1	13	1	2	16	8	14	92	70	2	28	--	111	1	367
Delaware	9	3	0	0	1	9	--	2	1	--	--	--	2	2	31
Elkhart	85	67	66	21	33	21	51	39	4	4	12	--	34	9	545
Fountain	23	38	46	3	9	39	18	45	8	--	14	--	8	4	274
Fulton	14	9	--	1	8	9	2	46	13	--	--	--	5	0	123
Grant	2	40	5	0	23	13	1	5	47	--	--	--	2	--	169
Hamilton	5	7	--	2	26	0	--	--	--	--	--	--	--	1	66
Hancock	2	27	--	1	4	15	1	8	3	7	--	--	2	--	75
Hendricks	28	12	14	0	1	--	1	0	--	--	--	--	--	7	75
Henry	4	10	--	0	1	--	0	5	11	--	6	--	4	--	45
Howard	6	11	1	0	2	13	1	9	5	--	5	--	1	7	67
Huntington	6	27	14	1	30	15	9	2	6	--	14	--	2	1	246
Jasper	10	2	--	1	5	--	25	17	39	--	--	--	--	--	99
Jay	1	7	1	0	27	19	20	30	56	--	--	--	--	--	207
Johnson	16	36	--	1	38	28	2	18	7	--	7	--	4	4	237
Kosciusko	41	45	147	17	22	80	93	91	128	9	62	0	15	21	1,031
La Grange	38	46	36	9	28	34	45	25	65	4	26	--	56	12	470
La Porte	86	21	--	0	2	0	26	94	2	--	--	--	23	0	255
Lake	5	1	--	1	1	--	--	1	40	--	--	--	--	--	51
Madison	7	1	--	0	1	2	3	7	1	--	--	0	2	--	55
Marion	0	12	--	1	3	5	2	0	0	--	10	--	18	2	73
Marshall	58	35	66	2	13	34	49	87	28	6	6	--	11	5	428
Miami	11	52	14	2	2	46	12	52	28	--	5	0	13	1	287
Montgomery	13	92	2	2	20	23	0	27	12	--	5	--	24	7	255
Newton	5	1	--	0	2	--	6	20	26	--	--	--	--	--	60
Noble	84	56	1	13	23	69	70	94	193	4	0	--	2	18	676
Porter	6	0	72	2	7	17	7	32	53	--	--	--	7	--	203
Pulaski	3	11	110	--	2	--	51	161	157	0	--	--	--	--	495

County	C1	C2	C3	C4	C5	C6	C7	C8	C9	C10	C11	C12	C13	C14	Total
Randolph	3	5	--	0	7	23	--	23	63	--	--	--	2	0	138
Rush	3	10	4	0	6	13	3	3	6	--	14	0	3	0	89
Shelby	0	2	45	0	--	13	1	--	19	--	7	--	--	--	102
St. Joseph	61	12	--	5	17	10	51	288	48	1	5	--	19	15	551
Starke	1	4	2	--	4	2	24	70	28	8	--	--	--	--	143
Steuben	44	90	51	15	34	24	19	107	115	4	45	--	114	11	746
Tippecanoe	0	31	--	1	13	--	2	35	4	--	--	--	2	3	102
Tipton	--	0	11	--	--	--	2	--	--	--	--	--	--	2	17
Wabash	14	20	0	2	12	32	8	59	16	--	2	--	0	2	232
Warren	7	13	--	1	0	3	--	10	62	--	19	--	45	0	169
Wayne	2	7	--	0	7	3	0	10	3	--	2	--	2	--	39
Wells	0	29	--	0	5	11	2	6	105	--	3	--	1	--	191
White	3	4	23	0	4	0	13	65	21	--	--	--	0	--	144
Whitley	23	34	67	11	37	91	3	15	35	4	14	0	8	12	398
Unit total	824	1,170	861	141	635	973	844	2,228	2,015	82	384	1	671	154	12,904
Upland Flats Unit															
Dearborn	17	38	--	3	34	13	3	115	110	--	7	--	2	5	391
Fayette	30	10	--	1	8	13	1	9	22	--	14	--	53	3	217
Franklin	14	25	14	3	47	24	10	148	105	3	31	--	87	5	564
Jefferson	11	74	--	2	36	36	52	211	42	67	22	0	152	2	791
Jennings	32	22	0	1	85	47	56	180	320	32	39	--	461	3	1,426
Ohio	4	1	--	0	0	2	--	11	5	--	--	--	6	0	56
Ripley	34	20	--	1	44	84	40	77	175	89	38	--	110	9	825
Switzerland	1	27	--	1	20	2	5	2	17	--	6	--	1	3	98
Union	22	6	1	1	25	9	--	6	5	--	17	--	1	1	107
Unit total	165	222	15	13	300	230	168	761	802	191	174	0	873	31	4,475
State total	2,346	3,031	1,437	256	4,493	4,799	2,549	12,252	10,690	488	1,637	34	11,087	1,516	62,573

All table cells without observations are indicated by — . Table value of 0 indicates the volume rounds to less than 1 thousand cubic feet. Columns and rows may not add to their totals due to rounding.

Table 8.—Industrial roundwood production by Forest Inventory Unit, species group, and product, Indiana, 2008

ALL UNITS

Species group	All products	Saw logs			Veneer logs			Pulp and composite products		Cooperage			Handles			Cabin logs	Excelsior/ shaving	Mine timbers
	MCF[a]	Int. 1/4 MBF[b]	Doyle MBF[c]	MCF[a]	Int. 1/4 MBF[b]	Doyle MBF[c]	MCF[a]	Cords[d]	MCF[a]	Int. 1/4 MBF[b]	Doyle MBF[c]	MCF[a]	Int. 1/4 MBF[b]	Doyle MBF[c]	MCF[a]	MCF[a]	MCF[a]	MCF[a]
Softwoods																		
Eastern redcedar	86	315	228	67	6	5	1	--	--	--	--	--	--	--	--	18	--	--
Loblolly/shortleaf pine	40	177	128	31	24	21	3	31	3	--	--	--	--	--	--	--	3	--
Red pine	7	0	0	0	--	--	--	--	--	--	--	--	--	--	--	7	--	--
White pine	640	1,751	1,269	304	14	12	2	295	25	--	--	--	--	--	--	304	7	--
Other pine	494	2,501	1,812	434	--	--	--	305	26	--	--	--	--	--	--	29	3	--
Softwood total	1,266	4,743	3,437	836	43	49	6	631	54	--	--	--	--	--	--	357	13	--
Hardwoods																		
Ash	4,292	22,507	16,309	3,698	127	111	17	4,466	353	--	--	--	1,272	922	206	7	--	10
Aspen/balsam poplar	44	266	193	44	--	--	--	--	--	--	--	--	--	--	--	--	--	--
Basswood	620	3,738	2,709	614	2	2	0	72	6	--	--	--	--	--	--	--	--	--
Beech	999	5,946	4,309	977	117	103	16	77	6	--	--	--	--	--	--	--	--	--
White birch	2	--	--	--	11	10	2	--	--	--	--	--	--	--	--	--	--	--
Other birch	2	--	--	--	--	--	--	25	2	--	--	--	--	--	--	--	--	--
Black cherry	2,346	12,468	9,035	2,048	1,716	1,505	235	797	63	--	--	--	--	--	--	--	--	--
Black walnut	3,031	16,294	11,807	2,495	2,939	2,578	414	1,546	122	--	--	--	--	--	--	--	--	--
Cottonwood	1,437	8,941	6,479	1,388	35	31	5	623	49	--	--	--	--	--	--	--	--	--
Elm	256	1,323	959	217	--	--	--	431	34	--	--	--	--	--	--	--	--	--
Hickory	4,493	25,408	18,412	4,175	635	557	87	2,648	209	--	--	--	138	100	22	57	--	--
Hard maple	4,799	25,587	18,541	4,358	1,890	1,658	259	1,595	126	--	--	--	0	0	0	--	--	--
Soft maple	2,549	14,221	10,305	2,422	135	118	18	1,370	108	--	--	--	--	--	--	--	--	--
Red oak group	12,252	67,579	48,970	11,434	2,667	2,339	365	5,049	399	--	--	--	--	--	--	43	--	10
White oak group	10,690	48,500	35,145	8,206	4,362	3,826	597	996	79	10,910	9,570	1,798	--	--	--	--	--	10
Sweetgum	488	2,876	2,084	473	--	--	--	58	5	--	--	--	--	--	--	--	--	10
Sycamore	1,637	8,538	6,187	1,403	--	--	--	2,836	224	--	--	--	--	--	--	--	--	10
Tupelo	34	175	127	29	6	5	1	59	5	--	--	--	--	--	--	--	--	10
Yellow-poplar	11,087	63,968	46,354	10,510	1,938	1,700	265	3,943	312	--	--	--	0	0	0	--	--	--
Other hardwoods	1,516	7,938	5,752	1,304	54	47	7	2,313	183	--	--	--	2	1	0	21	--	--
Hardwood total	62,573	336,274	243,677	55,794	16,635	14,592	2,288	28,903	2,283	10,910	9,570	1,798	1,413	1,024	229	129	--	52
State total	63,839	341,017	247,114	56,630	16,678	14,630	2,294	29,534	2,337	10,910	9,570	1,798	1,413	1,024	229	486	13	52

36

KNOBS UNIT

Species group	All products MCF[a]	Saw logs Int. 1/4 MBF[b]	Saw logs Doyle MBF[c]	Saw logs MCF[a]	Veneer logs Int. 1/4 MBF[b]	Veneer logs Doyle MBF[c]	Veneer logs MCF[a]	Pulp and composite products Cords[d]	Pulp and composite products MCF[a]	Cooperage Int. 1/4 MBF[b]	Cooperage Doyle MBF[c]	Cooperage MCF[a]	Handles Int. 1/4 MBF[b]	Handles Doyle MBF[c]	Handles MCF[a]	Cabin logs MCF[a]	Excelsior/ shaving MCF[a]	Mine timbers MCF[a]
Softwoods																		
Eastern redcedar	46	146	106	31	3	3	0	--	--	--	--	--	--	--	--	15	--	--
Loblolly/shortleaf pine	35	157	114	27	20	18	3	30	3	--	--	--	--	--	--	--	3	--
Red pine	0	--	0	0	--	--	--	--	--	--	--	--	--	--	--	--	--	--
White pine	402	1,474	1,068	256	--	--	--	289	25	--	--	--	--	--	--	118	3	--
Other pine	466	2,407	1,744	418	14	12	2	303	26	--	--	--	--	--	--	18	2	--
Softwood total	949	4,184	3,032	733	37	32	5	622	53	--	--	--	--	--	--	151	8	--
Hardwoods																		
Ash	1,628	9,267	6,715	1,523	34	30	5	262	21				496	359	80			--
Aspen/balsam poplar	32	196	142	32	--	--	--	--	--				--	--	--			--
Basswood	43	258	187	42	2	2	0	--	--				--	--	--			--
Beech	609	3,572	2,588	587	117	103	16	70	6				--	--	--			--
White birch	0	--	--	--	2	2	0	--	--				--	--	--			--
Black cherry	915	5,020	3,638	825	617	541	84	68	5				--	--	--			--
Black walnut	957	5,540	4,014	848	737	646	104	62	5				--	--	--			--
Cottonwood	142	911	660	141	--	--	--	1	0				--	--	--			--
Elm	49	278	201	46	14	12	2	20	2				--	--	--			--
Hickory	2,308	13,451	9,747	2,210	471	413	64	263	21				80	58	13	45		--
Hard maple	2,658	14,270	10,341	2,430	1,141	1,001	156	332	26				0	0	0			--
Soft maple	797	4,404	3,191	750	124	109	17	382	30				--	--	--			--
Red oak group	6,549	37,233	26,980	6,300	1,499	1,315	205	221	17				--	--	--	26		--
White oak group	6,691	27,678	20,057	4,683	2,703	2,371	370	424	33	9,738	8,542	1,605	--	--	--			--
Sweetgum	152	897	650	147	--	--	--	57	4				--	--	--			--
Sycamore	583	3,475	2,518	571	--	--	--	149	12				--	--	--			--
Tupelo	21	114	83	19	1	1	0	25	2				--	--	--			--
Yellow-poplar	6,242	36,779	26,651	6,043	1,243	1,090	170	375	30				0	0	0			--
Other hardwoods	701	4,059	2,941	667	21	18	3	219	17				1	1	0	14		--
Hardwood total	31,076	167,401	121,305	27,864	8,727	7,655	1,197	2,930	231	9,738	8,542	1,605	577	418	94	85	--	--
Unit total	32,025	171,585	124,337	28,596	8,764	7,688	1,202	3,552	284	9,738	8,542	1,605	577	418	94	236	8	--

(Table 8 continued on next page)

Table 8.—continued

LOWER WABASH UNIT

Species group	All products MCF[a]	Saw logs Int. 1/4 MBF[b]	Saw logs Doyle MBF[c]	Saw logs MCF[a]	Veneer logs Int. 1/4 MBF[b]	Veneer logs Doyle MBF[c]	Veneer logs MCF[a]	Pulp and composite products Cords[d]	Pulp and composite products MCF[a]	Cooperage Int. 1/4 MBF[b]	Cooperage Doyle MBF[c]	Cooperage MCF[a]	Handles Int. 1/4 MBF[b]	Handles Doyle MBF[c]	Handles MCF[a]	Cabin logs MCF[a]	Excelsior/ shaving MCF[a]	Mine timbers MCF[a]
Softwoods																		
Eastern redcedar	1	2	1	0	--	--	--	--	--	--	--	--	--	--	--	0	--	--
Loblolly/shortleaf pine	4	19	14	3	3	3	0	1	0	--	--	--	--	--	--	--	0	--
White pine	160	109	79	19	--	--	--	6	0	--	--	--	--	--	--	136	4	--
Other pine	26	81	59	14	--	--	1	1	0	--	--	--	--	--	--	11	1	--
Softwood total	191	212	154	37	3	3	0	8	1	--	--	--	--	--	--	148	5	--
Hardwoods																		
Ash	1,010	3,903	2,828	641	25	22	3	4,172	330	--	--	--	153	111	25	--	--	10
Aspen/balsam poplar	0	1	1	0	--	--	--	--	--	--	--	--	--	--	--	--	--	--
Basswood	51	278	201	46	--	--	--	69	5	--	--	--	--	--	--	--	--	--
Beech	128	777	563	128	--	--	--	6	1	--	--	--	--	--	--	--	--	--
White birch	1	--	--	--	9	8	1	--	0	--	--	--	--	--	--	--	--	--
Other birch	2	--	--	--	--	--	--	25	2	--	--	--	--	--	--	--	--	--
Black cherry	443	2,105	1,525	346	291	255	40	724	57	--	--	--	--	--	--	--	--	--
Black walnut	682	2,996	2,171	459	754	661	106	1,481	117	--	--	--	--	--	--	--	--	--
Cottonwood	496	1,666	1,207	274	--	--	--	2,686	212	--	--	--	--	--	--	--	--	10
Elm	420	2,452	1,777	381	--	--	--	494	39	--	--	--	--	--	--	--	--	--
Hickory	54	121	88	20	14	12	2	404	32	--	--	--	--	--	--	--	--	--
Hard maple	1,250	6,386	4,628	1,049	62	54	8	2,382	188	--	--	--	30	22	5	--	--	--
Soft maple	939	4,646	3,367	791	263	231	36	1,258	99	--	--	--	0	0	0	12	--	--
Red oak group	739	3,896	2,823	663	3	3	0	954	75	--	--	--	--	--	--	--	--	--
White oak group	2,714	13,313	9,647	2,253	443	389	61	4,822	381	--	--	--	--	--	--	10	--	10
Sweetgum	1,182	6,049	4,383	1,023	554	486	76	572	45	167	146	28	--	--	--	--	--	10
Sycamore	62	315	228	52	--	--	--	1	0	--	--	--	--	--	--	--	--	--
Tupelo	12	59	43	10	--	--	--	35	3	--	--	--	--	--	--	--	--	10
Yellow-poplar	3,300	17,918	12,984	2,944	540	474	74	3,568	282	--	--	--	0	0	0	--	--	--
Other hardwoods	631	2,787	2,020	458	18	16	2	2,059	163	--	--	--	0	0	0	8	--	--
Hardwood total	14,117	69,669	50,485	11,537	2,976	2,611	410	25,714	2,031	167	146	28	184	133	30	29	--	52
Unit total	14,309	69,880	50,638	11,574	2,980	2,614	411	25,722	2,032	167	146	28	184	133	30	177	5	52

38

Species group	All products MCF[a]	Saw logs Int. 1/4 MBF[b]	Saw logs Doyle MBF[c]	Saw logs MCF[a]	Veneer logs Int. 1/4 MBF[b]	Veneer logs Doyle MBF[c]	Veneer logs MCF[a]	Pulp and composite products Cords[d]	Pulp and composite products MCF[a]	Cooperage Int. 1/4 MBF[b]	Cooperage Doyle MBF[c]	Cooperage MCF[a]	Handles Int. 1/4 MBF[b]	Handles Doyle MBF[c]	Handles MCF[a]	Cabin logs MCF[a]	Excelsior/ shaving MCF[a]	Mine timbers MCF[a]
Softwoods																		
Red pine	7	--	--		--	--	--	--	--	--	--	--	--	--	--	7	--	--
White pine	49	3	2	0	--	--	--	--	--	--	--	--	--	--	--	49	--	--
Softwood total	56	3	2	0	--	--	--	--	--	--	--	--	--	--	--	56	--	--
Hardwoods																		
Ash	1,299	7,606	5,512	1,250	47	41	6	31	2	--	--	--	207	150	34	7	--	--
Aspen/balsam poplar	11	69	50	11	--	--	--	--	--	--	--	--	--	--	--	--	--	--
Basswood	446	2,711	1,964	445	--	--	--	3	0	--	--	--	--	--	--	--	--	--
Beech	166	1,007	730	166	--	--	--	0	0	--	--	--	--	--	--	--	--	--
Black cherry	824	4,487	3,251	737	630	553	86	5	0	--	--	--	--	--	--	--	--	--
Black walnut	1,170	6,964	5,046	1,066	734	644	103	2	0	--	--	--	--	--	--	--	--	--
Cottonwood	861	5,480	3,971	850	--	--	--	128	10	--	--	--	--	--	--	--	--	--
Elm	141	848	614	139	5	4	1	7	1	--	--	--	--	--	--	--	--	--
Hickory	635	3,780	2,739	621	88	77	12	3	0	--	--	--	8	6	1	--	--	--
Hard maple	973	5,466	3,961	931	305	268	42	5	0	--	--	--	--	--	--	--	--	--
Soft maple	844	4,942	3,581	842	--	--	--	34	3	--	--	--	--	--	--	--	--	--
Red oak group	2,228	12,691	9,196	2,147	534	468	73	6	0	--	--	--	--	--	--	--	--	--
White oak group	2,015	11,397	8,259	1,928	631	554	86	0	0	--	--	--	--	--	--	7	--	--
Sweetgum	82	502	364	82	--	--	--	1	--	--	--	--	--	--	--	--	--	--
Sycamore	384	2,340	1,696	384	5	4	--	1	0	--	--	--	--	--	--	--	--	--
Tupelo	1	--	--	--	--	--	--	--	--	--	--	--	--	--	--	--	--	--
Yellow-poplar	671	4,085	2,960	671	2	2	0	0	0	--	--	--	--	--	--	--	--	--
Other hardwoods	154	917	664	151	2	2	0	34	3	--	--	--	--	--	--	--	--	--
Hardwood total	12,904	75,292	54,559	12,423	2,984	2,618	411	259	20	--	--	--	215	156	35	14	--	--
Unit total	12,960	75,295	54,562	12,424	2,984	2,618	411	259	20	--	--	--	215	156	35	70	--	--

(Table 8 continued on next page)

39

Table 8.—continued

UPLAND FLATS UNIT

Species group	All products	Saw logs			Veneer logs			Pulp and composite products		Cooperage			Handles			Cabin logs	Excelsior/ shaving	Mine timbers
	MCF[a]	Int. 1/4 MBF[b]	Doyle MBF[c]	MCF[a]	Int. 1/4 MBF[b]	Doyle MBF[c]	MCF[a]	Cords[d]	MCF[a]	Int. 1/4 MBF[b]	Doyle MBF[c]	MCF[a]	Int. 1/4 MBF[b]	Doyle MBF[c]	MCF[a]	MCF[a]	MCF[a]	MCF[a]
Softwoods																		
Eastern redcedar	39	167	121	36	3	3	0	--	--	--	--	--	--	--	--	3	--	--
White pine	29	165	120	29	--	--	--	--	--	--	--	--	--	--	--	--	--	--
Other pine	2	13	9	2	--	--	--	--	--	--	--	--	--	--	--	--	--	--
Softwood total	70	345	250	66	3	3	0	--	--	--	--	--	--	--	--	3	--	--
Hardwoods																		
Ash	354	1,730	1,254	284	22	19	3	--	--	--	--	--	415	301	67	--	--	--
Basswood	81	491	356	81	--	--	--	--	--	--	--	--	--	--	--	--	--	--
Beech	97	589	427	97	--	--	--	--	--	--	--	--	--	--	--	--	--	--
White birch	0	--	--	0	0	0	0	--	--	--	--	--	--	--	--	--	--	--
Black cherry	165	855	620	141	178	156	24	--	--	--	--	--	--	--	--	--	--	--
Black walnut	222	795	576	122	713	625	100	--	--	--	--	--	--	--	--	--	--	--
Cottonwood	15	98	71	15	--	--	--	--	--	--	--	--	--	--	--	--	--	--
Elm	13	77	56	13	2	2	0	--	--	--	--	--	--	--	--	--	--	--
Hickory	300	1,791	1,298	294	14	12	2	--	--	--	--	--	21	15	3	--	--	--
Hard maple	230	1,205	873	205	180	158	25	--	--	--	--	--	0	0	0	--	--	--
Soft maple	168	980	710	167	7	6	1	--	--	--	--	--	--	--	--	--	--	--
Red oak group	761	4,342	3,146	735	191	168	26	--	--	--	--	--	--	--	--	--	--	--
White oak group	802	3,376	2,446	571	474	416	65	--	--	1,005	882	166	--	--	--	--	--	--
Sweetgum	191	1,162	842	191	--	--	--	--	--	--	--	--	--	--	--	--	--	--
Sycamore	174	1,058	767	174	--	--	--	--	--	--	--	--	--	--	--	--	--	--
Tupelo	0	1	1	0	--	--	--	--	--	--	--	--	--	--	--	--	--	--
Yellow-poplar	873	5,186	3,758	852	153	134	21	--	--	--	--	--	--	--	--	--	--	--
Other hardwoods	31	175	127	29	13	11	2	--	--	--	--	--	0	0	0	--	--	--
Hardwood total	4,475	23,912	17,328	3,970	1,947	1,708	269	--	--	1,005	882	166	436	316	71	--	--	--
Unit total	4,545	24,257	17,578	4,036	1,950	1,711	270	--	--	1,005	882	166	436	316	71	3	--	--

[a] Thousand cubic feet.
[b] Thousand board feet, International 1/4-inch rule.
[c] Thousand board feet, Doyle log rule.
[d] Standard cords are 128 cubic feet, consisting of 79 cubic feet of wood and 49 cubic feet of bark and air space.
All table cells without observations are indicated by – . Table value of 0 indicates the volume rounds to less than 1/2 unit of measure.
Columns and rows may not add to their totals due to rounding.

Table 9a.—Saw log receipts and production, in thousand board feet, International ¼-inch rule, by Forest Inventory Unit and species group, Indiana, 2005 and 2008

Species group	Receipts			Production		
	2005	2008	Percent change	2005	2008	Percent change
Softwoods						
Eastern redcedar	134	274	104%	133	315	137%
Loblolly/shortleaf pine	145	188	30%	145	177	22%
Red pine	--	0	--	--	0	--
White pine	2,423	1,779	-27%	2,141	1,751	-18%
Other pine	86	2,522	2833%	86	2,501	2808%
Softwood total	2,788	4,763	71%	2,505	4,743	89%
Hardwoods						
Ash	23,713	24,789	5%	20,766	22,507	8%
Aspen/balsam poplar	95	385	305%	86	266	209%
Basswood	3,666	4,077	11%	3,083	3,738	21%
Beech	8,656	6,129	-29%	7,842	5,946	-24%
Yellow birch	--	33	--	--	--	--
Other birch	10	--	--	10	--	--
Black cherry	17,150	15,446	-10%	13,801	12,468	-10%
Black walnut	20,264	17,035	-16%	18,588	16,294	-12%
Cottonwood	13,449	9,336	-31%	12,840	8,941	-30%
Elm	1,329	1,720	29%	1,174	1,323	13%
Hickory	30,598	27,395	-10%	27,171	25,408	-6%
Hard maple	40,595	27,955	-31%	36,035	25,587	-29%
Soft maple	26,535	16,898	-36%	22,361	14,221	-36%
Red oak group	106,120	73,012	-31%	95,918	67,579	-30%
White oak group	62,529	60,497	-3%	54,147	48,500	-10%
Sweetgum	5,214	2,943	-44%	5,047	2,876	-43%
Sycamore	9,831	8,765	-11%	8,959	8,538	-5%
Tupelo	41	158	285%	33	175	430%
Yellow-poplar	79,236	66,581	-16%	74,194	63,968	-14%
Other hardwoods	2,413	8,696	260%	2,228	7,938	256%
Hardwood total	451,444	371,848	-18%	404,284	336,274	-17%
State total	454,232	376,611	-17%	406,789	341,017	-16%

All table cells without observations are indicated by -- . Table value of 0 indicates the volume rounds to less than 1 thousand board feet. Columns and rows may not add to their totals due to rounding.

Table 9b.—Saw log receipts and production, in thousand board feet, Doyle rule, by Forest Inventory Unit and species group, Indiana, 2005 and 2008

Species group	Receipts			Production		
	2005	2008	Percent change	2005	2008	Percent change
Softwoods						
Eastern redcedar	97	199	104%	96	228	137%
Loblolly/shortleaf pine	105	136	30%	105	128	22%
Red pine	--	0	--	--	0	--
White pine	1,756	1,289	-27%	1,551	1,269	-18%
Other pine	62	1,828	2833%	62	1,812	2808%
Softwood total	2,020	3,451	71%	1,815	3,437	89%
Hardwoods						
Ash	17,183	17,963	5%	15,048	16,309	8%
Aspen/balsam poplar	69	279	305%	62	193	209%
Basswood	2,657	2,954	11%	2,234	2,709	21%
Beech	6,272	4,441	-29%	5,683	4,309	-24%
Yellow birch	--	24	--	--	--	--
Other birch	7	--	--	7	--	--
Black cherry	12,428	11,193	-10%	10,001	9,035	-10%
Black walnut	14,684	12,344	-16%	13,470	11,807	-12%
Cottonwood	9,746	6,765	-31%	9,304	6,479	-30%
Elm	963	1,246	29%	851	959	13%
Hickory	22,172	19,851	-10%	19,689	18,412	-6%
Hard maple	29,417	20,257	-31%	26,112	18,541	-29%
Soft maple	19,228	12,245	-36%	16,204	10,305	-36%
Red oak group	76,899	52,907	-31%	69,506	48,970	-30%
White oak group	45,311	43,838	-3%	39,237	35,145	-10%
Sweetgum	3,778	2,133	-44%	3,657	2,084	-43%
Sycamore	7,124	6,351	-11%	6,492	6,187	-5%
Tupelo	30	114	285%	24	127	430%
Yellow-poplar	57,417	48,247	-16%	53,764	46,354	-14%
Other hardwoods	1,749	6,301	260%	1,614	5,752	256%
Hardwood total	327,133	269,455	-18%	292,959	243,677	-17%
State total	329,154	272,907	-17%	294,775	247,114	-16%

All table cells without observations are indicated by --. Table value of 0 indicates the volume rounds to less than 1 thousand board feet. Columns and rows may not add to their totals due to rounding.

Table 10.—Wood material harvested for industrial roundwood, in thousand cubic feet, by Forest Inventory Unit, source of material, and species group, Indiana, 2008[a]

ALL UNITS

	Source of material												
	Growing stock				Non-growing stock								
	Used for products				Used for products								
Species group	Sawtimber	Pole-timber	Logging residue (not used)	Total growing stock	Limbwood	Cull trees	Dead trees	Nonforest trees	Logging slash (not used)	Total non-growing stock	Total used	Total not used	Total harvested
Softwoods													
Eastern redcedar	85.4	--	0.6	86.0	--	0.6	--	--	47.5	48.1	86.0	48.1	134.1
Shortleaf pine	37.3	2.1	4.1	43.4	--	0.1	--	--	40.3	40.3	39.4	44.3	83.7
Red pine	7.0	--	0.7	7.7	--	0.0	--	--	9.0	9.0	7.0	9.7	16.7
White pine	619.3	17.4	66.0	702.7	--	1.2	--	--	785.1	786.2	637.9	851.1	1,488.9
Other pine	473.7	17.7	50.4	541.8	--	1.0	--	--	600.3	601.3	492.3	650.8	1,143.1
Softwood total	1,222.6	37.1	121.8	1,381.6	--	2.8	--	--	1,482.1	1,485.0	1,262.6	1,604.0	2,866.6
Hardwoods													
Ash	3,901.0	62.0	1,265.3	5,228.3	206.8	83.5	38.3	--	2,406.1	2,734.7	4,291.5	3,671.4	7,963.0
Aspen/balsam poplar	41.6	--	12.9	54.6	1.7	0.0	0.4	--	28.3	30.5	43.8	41.2	85.0
Basswood	587.7	0.2	181.9	769.9	24.9	1.3	6.0	--	397.1	429.3	620.1	579.0	1,199.2
Beech	948.6	0.2	291.6	1,240.5	39.1	1.6	9.6	--	632.5	682.8	999.1	924.1	1,923.2
White birch	1.5	--	0.2	1.7	0.1	0.3	--	--	0.1	0.1	1.5	0.3	1.8
Other birch	1.2	0.1	0.1	1.4	0.3	0.3	0.0	--	0.0	0.7	2.0	0.1	2.1
Black cherry	2,221.3	2.5	643.5	2,867.2	90.6	11.4	20.3	--	1,339.1	1,461.5	2,346.2	1,982.6	4,328.7
Black walnut	2,519.3	4.8	231.6	2,755.8	66.6	86.6	0.8	--	366.8	873.5	3,030.9	598.4	3,629.3
Cottonwood	1,398.4	1.9	205.7	1,606.1	22.8	13.3	0.3	352.7	786.0	822.4	1,436.8	991.7	2,428.5
Elm	232.6	1.3	66.3	300.3	14.3	5.6	2.3	--	141.5	163.8	256.3	207.8	464.1
Hickory	4,200.7	12.8	1,272.4	5,485.9	198.6	38.9	42.0	--	2,708.0	2,987.5	4,493.0	3,980.3	8,473.4
Hard maple	4,520.8	5.0	1,204.9	5,730.7	223.9	48.9	0.8	--	2,625.6	2,899.2	4,799.4	3,830.5	8,629.9
Soft maple	2,380.8	4.2	644.0	3,029.1	129.6	33.2	0.7	--	1,433.9	1,597.3	2,548.5	2,077.9	4,626.4
Red oak group	11,290.8	21.8	3,258.9	14,571.5	518.1	126.8	294.2	--	6,406.1	7,345.2	12,251.8	9,664.9	21,916.7
White oak group	9,907.5	9.3	2,810.2	12,726.9	342.0	222.3	209.0	--	4,627.3	5,400.6	10,690.0	7,437.5	18,127.5
Sweetgum	453.5	6.3	140.8	600.6	21.0	2.2	4.6	--	305.7	333.5	487.6	446.5	934.1
Sycamore	1,474.0	15.0	424.3	1,913.3	95.0	38.3	15.1	--	911.5	1,059.8	1,637.3	1,335.8	2,973.1
Tupelo	31.1	0.2	8.8	40.0	1.9	0.8	0.3	--	18.7	21.7	34.2	27.5	61.7
Yellow-poplar	10,450.2	12.2	3,160.4	13,622.8	463.0	56.9	104.3	--	6,815.2	7,439.5	11,086.6	9,975.7	21,062.3
Other hardwoods	1,381.3	7.2	400.4	1,788.9	83.1	30.4	14.1	--	861.1	988.7	1,516.1	1,261.5	2,777.6
Hardwood total	57,943.8	167.0	16,224.4	74,335.3	2,543.4	802.4	763.2	352.7	32,810.4	37,272.2	62,572.6	49,034.9	111,607.5
State total	59,166.4	204.2	16,346.3	75,716.9	2,543.4	805.3	763.2	352.7	34,292.6	38,757.2	63,835.2	50,638.8	114,474.0

(Table 10 continued on next page)

Table 10.—continued

KNOBS UNIT

| | Growing stock | | | | Non-growing stock | | | | | | | | |
| | Used for products | | | | Used for products | | | | | | | | |
Species group	Sawtimber	Pole-timber	Logging residue (not used)	Total growing stock	Limbwood	Cull trees	Dead trees	Nonforest trees	Logging slash (not used)	Total non-growing stock	Total used	Total not used	Total harvested
Softwoods													
Eastern redcedar	45.8	--	0.3	46.1	--	0.3	--	--	25.5	25.5	46.1	25.8	71.9
Shortleaf pine	33.0	1.9	3.6	38.5	--	0.1	--	--	35.9	36.0	35.0	39.5	74.5
Red pine	0.0	--	0.0	0.0	--	0.0	--	--	0.0	0.0	0.0	0.0	0.1
White pine	382.4	16.7	40.6	439.7	--	0.9	--	--	486.2	487.0	399.9	526.8	926.7
Other pine	445.5	17.5	47.4	510.4	--	1.0	--	--	565.2	566.2	463.9	612.6	1,076.6
Softwood total	906.6	36.2	91.9	1,034.8	--	2.2	--	--	1,112.8	1,115.0	945.0	1,204.7	2,149.8
Hardwoods													
Ash	1,520.1	17.2	511.4	2,048.7	62.9	13.2	15.0	--	986.1	1,077.1	1,628.3	1,497.5	3,125.8
Aspen/balsam poplar	30.6	--	9.5	40.1	1.3	0.0	0.3	--	20.8	22.4	32.2	30.3	62.4
Basswood	40.5	--	12.6	53.1	1.6	0.0	0.4	--	27.4	29.5	42.6	39.9	82.6
Beech	577.5	0.2	176.2	753.9	23.8	1.3	5.8	--	380.4	411.2	608.5	556.6	1,165.1
White birch	0.2	--	0.0	0.3	--	--	--	--	0.0	0.0	0.2	0.1	0.3
Black cherry	871.9	0.2	256.8	1,129.0	33.1	1.4	8.1	--	538.2	580.7	914.6	795.0	1,709.7
Black walnut	801.6	0.2	74.8	876.7	16.4	23.5	0.0	115.2	121.0	276.0	956.9	195.8	1,152.7
Cottonwood	139.5	0.0	20.8	160.3	1.5	0.6	0.0	--	80.0	82.1	141.5	100.8	242.3
Elm	46.3	0.1	13.9	60.2	2.0	0.3	0.5	--	29.7	32.5	49.1	43.5	92.7
Hickory	2,187.2	3.4	673.7	2,864.4	89.7	6.1	21.7	--	1,432.9	1,550.3	2,308.1	2,106.6	4,414.7
Hard maple	2,518.4	1.0	675.6	3,195.0	117.9	20.2	0.2	--	1,471.9	1,610.2	2,657.7	2,147.5	4,805.2
Soft maple	746.5	1.2	201.0	948.6	39.5	9.7	0.2	--	444.6	494.1	797.1	645.6	1,442.7
Red oak group	6,100.9	0.7	1,788.7	7,890.2	249.8	36.5	160.9	--	3,526.9	3,974.0	6,548.7	5,315.5	11,864.2
White oak group	6,198.9	1.3	1,748.0	7,948.3	194.3	177.4	119.2	--	2,652.2	3,143.1	6,691.1	4,400.3	11,091.4
Sweetgum	142.9	0.2	43.8	186.8	6.5	0.8	1.5	--	95.3	104.1	151.9	139.1	291.0
Sycamore	550.1	0.5	169.3	719.8	24.3	2.3	5.6	--	369.3	401.4	582.7	538.6	1,121.2
Tupelo	19.2	0.1	5.6	24.9	1.1	0.3	0.2	--	12.2	13.8	20.8	17.8	38.7
Yellow-poplar	5,933.2	1.2	1,814.1	7,748.4	240.5	8.5	59.0	--	3,916.5	4,224.4	6,242.4	5,730.5	11,972.9
Other hardwoods	661.1	0.7	202.7	864.5	29.5	3.2	6.7	--	440.6	480.1	701.3	643.3	1,344.6
Hardwood total	29,086.6	28.1	8,398.5	37,513.2	1,135.5	305.3	405.2	115.2	16,545.9	18,507.1	31,075.9	24,944.4	56,020.3
Unit total	29,993.2	64.3	8,490.4	38,548.0	1,135.5	307.6	405.2	115.2	17,658.7	19,622.1	32,021.0	26,149.1	58,170.1

44

LOWER WABASH UNIT

	Source of material												
	Growing stock				Non-growing stock								
	Used for products				Used for products								
Species group	Sawtimber	Pole-timber	Logging residue (not used)	Total growing stock	Limbwood	Cull trees	Dead trees	Nonforest trees	Logging slash (not used)	Total non-growing stock	Total used	Total not used	Total harvested
Softwoods													
Eastern redcedar	0.7	--	0.0	0.7	--	0.0	--	--	0.4	0.4	0.7	0.4	1.2
Shortleaf pine	4.3	0.1	0.5	4.9	--	0.0	--	--	4.4	4.4	4.4	4.8	9.2
White pine	159.0	0.7	17.0	176.7	--	0.2	--	--	199.0	199.2	159.9	216.0	375.9
Other pine	26.0	0.2	2.8	29.0	--	0.0	--	--	32.3	32.3	26.2	35.1	61.3
Softwood total	190.0	1.0	20.3	211.2	--	0.2	--	--	236.1	236.3	191.2	256.4	447.6
Hardwoods													
Ash	835.9	24.2	222.0	1,082.1	83.5	57.7	8.3	--	421.9	571.4	1,009.6	643.9	1,653.5
Aspen/balsam poplar	0.2	--	0.1	0.3	0.0	0.0	0.0	--	0.1	0.2	0.2	0.2	0.4
Basswood	46.8	0.2	13.7	60.8	2.7	0.9	0.5	--	29.7	33.8	51.2	43.4	94.6
Beech	121.7	0.0	37.8	159.5	5.1	0.2	1.2	--	82.6	89.0	128.2	120.4	248.6
White birch	1.2	--	0.2	1.4	--	--	--	--	0.1	0.1	1.2	0.3	1.5
Other birch	1.2	0.1	0.1	1.4	0.3	0.3	0.0	--	0.0	0.7	2.0	0.1	2.1
Black cherry	404.1	2.2	110.5	516.8	23.3	9.5	3.7	--	227.1	263.6	442.9	337.5	780.4
Black walnut	548.2	4.6	48.2	601.0	28.5	31.2	0.7	68.7	71.8	201.0	682.0	120.0	802.1
Cottonwood	399.4	1.5	57.4	458.3	10.6	7.8	0.2	--	216.1	234.8	419.6	273.5	693.0
Elm	40.6	1.3	7.4	49.2	6.3	5.2	0.4	--	13.6	25.4	53.7	20.9	74.6
Hickory	1,126.0	8.4	322.3	1,456.6	73.3	31.7	11.4	--	682.5	798.9	1,250.6	1,004.8	2,255.5
Hard maple	858.9	3.9	220.5	1,083.3	53.9	21.3	0.6	--	478.6	554.4	938.6	699.1	1,637.7
Soft maple	676.0	3.0	177.5	856.4	43.4	16.5	0.5	--	393.5	453.8	739.3	570.9	1,310.2
Red oak group	2,402.8	21.1	652.8	3,076.7	155.6	74.9	59.9	--	1,268.3	1,558.7	2,714.3	1,921.1	4,635.4
White oak group	1,082.2	7.9	304.9	1,395.1	49.6	16.4	26.3	--	574.6	666.9	1,182.5	879.5	2,061.9
Sweetgum	50.6	6.2	16.1	72.9	3.8	1.2	0.5	--	33.6	39.1	62.3	49.7	112.0
Sycamore	393.2	14.5	89.9	497.6	49.0	35.7	4.0	--	181.4	270.1	496.4	271.3	767.6
Tupelo	11.0	0.1	3.0	14.1	0.9	0.5	0.1	--	6.4	7.8	12.5	9.3	21.8
Yellow-poplar	3,047.5	11.1	892.6	3,951.2	163.2	47.5	30.5	--	1,912.9	2,154.1	3,299.7	2,805.6	6,105.2
Other hardwoods	545.9	6.4	144.3	696.6	46.1	26.7	5.6	--	304.3	382.6	630.7	448.6	1,079.2
Hardwood total	12,593.5	116.6	3,321.1	16,031.1	799.0	385.1	154.5	68.7	6,899.0	8,306.3	14,117.4	10,220.0	24,337.4
Unit total	12,783.4	117.6	3,341.3	16,242.3	799.0	385.3	154.5	68.7	7,135.0	8,542.6	14,308.5	10,476.4	24,784.9

(Table 10 continued on next page)

Table 10.—continued

NORTHERN UNIT

	Source of material												
	Growing stock				Non-growing stock								
	Used for products		Logging residue (not used)	Total growing stock	Used for products				Logging slash (not used)	Total non-growing stock	Total used	Total not used	Total harvested
Species group	Sawtimber	Pole-timber			Limbwood	Cull trees	Dead trees	Nonforest trees					
Softwoods													
Red pine	7.0	--	0.7	7.7	--	0.0	--	--	8.9	8.9	7.0	9.7	16.7
White pine	49.3	--	5.3	54.5	--	0.1	--	--	63.1	63.2	49.3	68.4	117.7
Softwood total	56.2	--	6.0	62.3	--	0.1	--	--	72.1	72.1	56.3	78.1	134.4
Hardwoods													
Ash	1,225.6	6.9	397.6	1,630.2	49.4	4.9	12.3	--	813.2	879.7	1,299.1	1,210.9	2,509.9
Aspen/balsam poplar	10.8	--	3.4	14.2	0.4	0.0	0.1	--	7.4	7.9	11.4	10.7	22.1
Basswood	423.6	0.0	131.8	555.3	17.4	0.3	4.3	--	287.9	309.9	445.6	419.6	865.3
Beech	157.4	0.0	49.0	206.3	6.5	0.1	1.6	--	107.0	115.2	165.5	155.9	321.5
Black cherry	787.3	0.0	231.0	1,018.3	28.8	0.5	7.2	--	481.5	518.0	823.8	712.5	1,536.3
Black walnut	980.3	0.0	92.0	1,072.3	19.5	28.6	0.0	141.3	149.7	339.2	1,169.8	241.7	1,411.5
Cottonwood	844.6	0.4	125.3	970.4	10.5	4.9	0.1	--	481.3	496.8	860.5	606.6	1,467.2
Elm	133.5	0.0	41.3	174.8	5.5	0.2	1.4	--	90.1	97.1	140.6	131.4	272.0
Hickory	603.5	0.3	186.5	790.2	24.2	0.6	6.0	--	402.1	433.0	634.6	588.6	1,223.2
Hard maple	924.3	0.0	251.2	1,175.5	42.7	6.1	0.0	--	552.4	601.1	973.1	803.5	1,776.6
Soft maple	799.3	0.1	221.5	1,021.0	39.0	5.9	0.0	--	497.2	542.1	844.3	718.8	1,563.1
Red oak group	2,077.7	0.0	609.5	2,687.1	84.1	11.5	54.8	--	1,201.3	1,351.7	2,228.1	1,810.7	4,038.8
White oak group	1,880.2	0.0	548.6	2,428.8	75.2	10.3	49.0	--	1,076.4	1,210.9	2,014.7	1,625.0	3,639.7
Sweetgum	78.4	--	24.4	102.8	3.2	0.1	0.8	--	53.3	57.4	82.5	77.7	160.2
Sycamore	365.5	0.0	113.7	479.2	15.0	0.2	3.7	--	248.5	267.4	384.5	362.2	746.7
Tupelo	0.7	--	0.1	0.9	--	--	--	--	0.0	0.0	0.7	0.2	0.9
Yellow-poplar	638.4	0.0	198.6	836.9	26.1	0.4	6.5	--	433.8	466.9	671.5	632.4	1,303.9
Other hardwoods	145.2	0.1	44.7	190.0	6.3	0.5	1.5	--	97.5	105.8	153.6	142.2	295.8
Hardwood total	12,076.3	7.9	3,270.1	15,354.3	454.0	75.0	149.3	141.3	6,980.6	7,800.3	12,903.9	10,250.7	23,154.6
Unit total	12,132.5	7.9	3,276.1	15,416.6	454.0	75.1	149.3	141.3	7,052.7	7,872.5	12,960.2	10,328.8	23,289.0

UPLAND FLATS UNIT

	Source of material												
	Growing stock				Non-growing stock								
	Used for products				Used for products								
Species group	Sawtimber	Pole-timber	Logging residue (not used)	Total growing stock	Limbwood	Cull trees	Dead trees	Nonforest trees	Logging slash (not used)	Total non-growing stock	Total used	Total not used	Total harvested
Softwoods													
Eastern redcedar	38.9	--	0.3	39.1	--	0.3	--	--	21.6	21.9	39.1	21.9	61.0
White pine	28.7	--	3.1	31.8	--	0.0	--	--	36.8	36.8	28.7	39.9	68.6
Other pine	2.2	--	0.2	2.4	--	0.0	--	--	2.8	2.8	2.2	3.0	5.2
Softwood total	69.7	--	3.6	73.3	--	0.3	--	--	61.2	61.5	70.0	64.8	134.8
Hardwoods													
Ash	319.3	13.7	134.3	467.3	11.1	7.6	2.8	--	184.9	206.4	354.5	319.3	673.7
Basswood	76.7	--	23.9	100.6	3.1	0.0	0.8	--	52.2	56.2	80.7	76.1	156.8
Beech	92.1	--	28.6	120.7	3.8	0.1	0.9	--	62.6	67.4	96.8	91.2	188.1
White birch	0.0	--	0.0	0.0	--	--	--	--	0.0	0.0	0.0	0.0	0.0
Black cherry	157.9	--	45.2	203.1	5.5	0.1	1.4	--	92.2	99.2	164.9	137.5	302.3
Black walnut	189.2	--	16.5	205.8	2.2	3.3	--	27.5	24.3	57.2	222.2	40.8	263.0
Cottonwood	14.9	--	2.2	17.2	0.2	0.1	--	--	8.6	8.8	15.1	10.8	25.9
Elm	12.3	--	3.8	16.0	0.5	0.0	0.1	--	8.1	8.8	12.9	11.9	24.8
Hickory	284.1	0.7	89.9	374.6	11.5	0.6	2.9	--	190.4	205.3	299.7	280.3	579.9
Hard maple	219.2	0.0	57.7	276.9	9.4	1.3	--	--	122.7	133.4	229.9	180.4	410.3
Soft maple	159.0	--	44.0	203.1	7.6	1.1	--	--	98.6	107.3	167.8	142.6	310.4
Red oak group	709.5	--	208.0	917.5	28.7	3.9	18.7	--	409.6	460.9	760.7	617.6	1,378.3
White oak group	746.1	--	208.7	954.8	22.9	18.2	14.5	--	324.1	379.7	801.7	532.8	1,334.5
Sweetgum	181.5	--	56.5	238.0	7.4	0.1	1.9	--	123.4	132.8	191.0	179.9	370.9
Sycamore	165.2	--	51.4	216.7	6.8	0.1	1.7	--	112.4	120.9	173.8	163.8	337.6
Tupelo	0.2	--	0.0	0.2	0.0	0.0	0.0	--	0.1	0.1	0.2	0.2	0.3
Yellow-poplar	831.1	--	255.2	1,086.3	33.2	0.5	8.3	--	552.0	594.0	873.1	807.2	1,680.3
Other hardwoods	29.1	0.0	8.8	37.9	1.1	0.0	0.3	--	18.7	20.1	30.5	27.5	58.0
Hardwood total	4,187.5	14.4	1,234.8	5,436.7	154.9	37.0	54.2	27.5	2,385.0	2,658.5	4,475.4	3,619.8	8,095.2
Unit total	4,257.2	14.4	1,238.4	5,510.0	154.9	37.3	54.2	27.5	2,446.2	2,720.0	4,545.5	3,684.5	8,230.0

[a] Based on factors obtained from regional utilization studies.

All table cells without observations are indicated by -- . Table value of 0.0 indicates the volume rounds to less than 0.1 thousand cubic feet. Columns and rows may not add to their totals due to rounding.

47

Table 11.—Growing-stock removals from timberland for industrial roundwood, in thousand cubic feet, by Forest Inventory Unit, county, and species group, Indiana, 2008

Forest Inventory Unit and county	All species	Softwoods						Hardwoods					
		Eastern redcedar	Loblolly/ shortleaf pine	Red pine	White pine	Other pine	Total softwoods	Ash	Aspen/ balsam poplar	Bass-wood	Beech	White birch	Other birch
Knobs Unit													
Brown	3,855	--	2	--	--	--	2	75	1	1	51	0	--
Clark	1,360	2	--	--	1	37	39	163	--	--	57	--	--
Crawford	2,288	3	6	--	--	7	16	42	--	--	5	--	--
Dubois	2,115	--	2	--	5	--	8	154	--	--	15	--	--
Floyd	591	1	--	--	--	10	10	51	--	--	0	--	--
Harrison	1,726	14	--	--	--	85	100	156	8	5	15	--	--
Jackson	3,244	1	--	0	130	88	220	276	8	1	114	0	--
Lawrence	3,350	0	3	--	107	--	110	103	19	--	65	--	--
Monroe	4,144	2	0	--	75	--	77	196	0	23	118	--	--
Morgan	1,872	--	--	--	--	--	--	206	1	12	61	--	--
Orange	3,317	5	6	--	79	16	106	106	2	0	44	--	--
Owen	2,182	0	--	--	--	3	3	135	1	11	60	--	--
Perry	1,826	4	18	--	43	1	65	36	--	--	27	--	--
Scott	607	8	--	--	--	71	79	4	--	--	17	--	--
Spencer	689	0	--	--	--	--	0	69	--	--	15	--	--
Warrick	796	--	2	--	--	--	2	43	--	--	14	--	--
Washington	4,585	5	--	--	--	192	197	236	--	0	74	--	--
Unit total	38,548	46	39	0	440	510	1,035	2,049	40	53	754	0	--
Lower Wabash Unit													
Clay	1,204	--	--	--	7	2	10	70	--	--	4	0	--
Daviess	858	--	--	--	--	--	--	46	--	--	1	--	--
Gibson	420	--	--	--	--	--	--	68	--	--	1	--	--
Greene	2,747	--	1	--	19	6	25	28	--	4	20	0	--
Knox	751	--	--	--	--	--	--	145	--	--	1	--	--
Martin	2,731	0	--	--	--	2	2	126	--	1	59	0	0
Parke	2,032	--	--	--	--	--	--	117	--	17	61	--	--
Pike	646	0	4	--	148	18	170	16	--	--	0	1	--
Posey	254	--	--	--	--	--	--	33	--	--	--	--	--
Putnam	1,763	--	--	--	--	--	--	133	--	12	12	--	--
Sullivan	1,662	--	--	--	3	1	4	235	--	2	0	0	1
Vanderburgh	156	--	--	--	--	--	--	14	--	--	1	--	--
Vermillion	232	--	--	--	--	--	--	4	0	5	--	1	--
Vigo	788	--	--	--	--	--	--	48	--	21	--	--	--
Unit total	16,242	1	5	--	177	29	211	1,082	0	61	160	1	1

Forest Inventory Unit and county	All species	Softwoods						Hardwoods					
		Eastern redcedar	Loblolly/ shortleaf pine	Red pine	White pine	Other pine	Total softwoods	Ash	Aspen/ balsam poplar	Bass- wood	Beech	White birch	Other birch
Northern Unit													
Adams	176	--	--	--	--	--	--	5	--	--	--	--	--
Allen	1,648	--	--	--	--	--	--	83	--	368	108	--	--
Bartholomew	414	--	--	--	--	--	--	17	1	--	23	--	--
Blackford	29	--	--	--	--	--	--	5	0	--	--	--	--
Boone	103	--	--	--	--	--	--	35	--	--	1	--	--
Carroll	282	--	--	--	--	--	--	10	--	9	4	--	--
Cass	276	--	--	--	--	--	--	25	--	2	--	--	--
Clinton	78	--	--	--	--	--	--	4	--	--	4	--	--
De Kalb	444	--	--	--	--	--	--	52	--	29	1	--	--
Decatur	447	--	--	--	--	--	--	9	--	--	3	--	--
Delaware	37	--	--	--	--	--	--	1	--	--	--	--	--
Elkhart	650	--	--	6	--	--	6	95	0	9	18	--	--
Fountain	318	--	--	--	--	--	--	20	--	1	1	--	--
Fulton	148	--	--	--	--	--	--	12	--	8	--	--	--
Grant	194	--	--	--	--	--	--	38	0	1	--	--	--
Hamilton	80	--	--	--	--	--	--	21	--	--	--	--	--
Hancock	85	--	--	--	--	--	--	16	--	--	--	--	--
Hendricks	87	--	--	--	--	--	--	14	--	0	--	--	--
Henry	52	--	--	--	--	--	--	1	--	2	--	--	--
Howard	78	--	--	--	--	--	--	12	--	1	--	--	--
Huntington	295	--	--	--	--	--	--	117	0	17	14	--	--
Jasper	119	--	--	--	--	--	--	--	--	3	1	--	--
Jay	251	--	--	--	--	--	--	55	0	3	1	--	--
Johnson	283	--	--	--	--	--	--	89	0	9	9	--	--
Kosciusko	1,238	--	--	--	--	--	--	296	0	17	9	--	--
La Grange	574	--	--	2	14	--	15	35	3	17	1	--	--
La Porte	305	--	--	--	--	--	--	1	--	--	--	--	--
Lake	62	--	--	--	--	--	--	2	1	--	--	--	--
Madison	67	--	--	--	--	--	--	37	--	3	--	--	--
Marion	89	--	--	--	--	--	--	27	--	0	--	--	--
Marshall	506	--	--	--	--	--	--	24	--	9	1	--	--
Miami	333	--	--	--	--	--	--	54	0	7	0	--	--
Montgomery	284	--	--	--	--	--	--	29	3	1	1	--	--
Newton	72	--	--	--	--	--	--	--	--	--	--	--	--
Noble	807	--	--	--	--	--	--	55	--	2	5	--	--

(Table 11 continued on the next page)

49

Table 11.—continued

County											
Porter	241	--	--	--	--	--	--	3	--	--	--	--
Pulaski	587	--	--	--	--	--	--	--	--	--	--	--
Randolph	166	--	--	--	--	--	--	14	--	--	1	--
Rush	107	--	--	--	--	--	--	32	--	--	--	--
Shelby	121	--	--	--	--	--	--	20	--	--	--	--
St. Joseph	667	--	--	--	--	--	--	18	--	5	--	--
Starke	171	--	--	--	--	--	--	--	--	--	--	--
Steuben	883	--	--	--	--	--	1	81	1	7	1	--
Tippecanoe	115	--	--	--	--	--	--	13	1	1	1	--
Tipton	12	--	--	--	--	--	--	1	--	--	--	--
Wabash	277	--	0	0	--	0	--	70	--	10	1	--
Warren	204	--	--	--	--	--	--	6	--	3	--	--
Wayne	45	--	--	--	--	--	--	4	--	--	--	--
Wells	224	--	--	--	--	--	--	34	--	0	--	--
White	171	--	--	--	--	--	--	6	--	5	--	--
Whitley	512	--	41	41	--	41	6	30	6	19	--	--
Unit total	**15,417**	**8**	**55**	**55**	**8**	**62**	**14**	**1,630**	**14**	**555**	**206**	**--**
Upland Flats Unit												
Dearborn	468	0	--	--	--	0	--	56	--	3	--	--
Fayette	270	0	--	--	--	0	--	72	--	--	0	--
Franklin	683	--	--	--	--	--	--	56	--	--	7	--
Jefferson	971	16	2	2	2	20	--	46	--	56	4	--
Jennings	1,779	8	29	29	--	37	--	98	--	17	71	0
Ohio	73	0	--	--	--	0	--	35	--	--	--	--
Ripley	1,014	8	--	--	--	8	--	72	--	24	37	--
Switzerland	122	8	--	--	--	8	--	18	--	--	--	--
Union	130	0	--	--	--	0	--	15	--	2	--	--
Unit total	**5,510**	**39**	**32**	**32**	**2**	**73**	**--**	**467**	**--**	**101**	**121**	**0**
State total	**75,717**	**86**	**43**	**703**	**8**	**542**	**1,382**	**5,228**	**55**	**770**	**1,240**	**2**

Forest Inventory Unit and county	Black cherry	Black walnut	Cotton-wood	Elm	Hickory	Hard maple	Soft maple	Red oak group	White oak group	Sweet-gum	Syca-more	Tupelo/gum	Yellow-poplar	Other hardwoods	Total hardwoods
Knobs Unit															
Brown	98	35	--	6	338	254	136	1,543	1,027	1	64	3	163	57	3,853
Clark	17	49	--	0	119	66	20	176	217	31	17	--	378	10	1,321
Crawford	74	20	--	5	258	182	18	572	761	--	61	2	241	33	2,273
Dubois	79	80	--	3	154	156	115	331	478	28	34	2	353	124	2,107
Floyd	10	10	--	--	22	44	8	101	305	0	--	0	14	15	581
Harrison	145	38	1	7	94	236	27	419	197	--	6	1	217	54	1,627
Jackson	83	46	11	3	117	281	153	444	426	53	165	2	802	40	3,024
Lawrence	164	69	5	7	145	216	55	757	386	--	139	1	1,023	87	3,240
Monroe	162	236	--	7	463	237	74	709	828	6	29	0	897	79	4,066
Morgan	21	40	99	1	130	208	71	397	116	--	23	1	444	41	1,872
Orange	49	86	--	4	149	320	27	806	607	9	53	2	803	144	3,212
Owen	9	22	3	3	156	232	56	259	170	2	8	2	1,013	37	2,179
Perry	20	14	--	5	203	208	60	381	560	12	11	3	193	28	1,761
Scott	16	26	--	0	30	107	5	7	171	2	2	3	126	11	527
Spencer	47	15	--	1	117	33	58	125	110	23	23	--	8	44	689
Warrick	6	8	41	1	71	27	53	332	86	20	38	1	33	22	794
Washington	130	81	--	7	297	387	14	530	1,504	--	48	1	1,040	39	4,388
Unit total	1,129	877	160	60	2,864	3,195	949	7,890	7,948	187	720	25	7,748	864	37,513
Lower Wabash Unit															
Clay	36	37	--	3	49	94	130	414	62	3	39	--	240	12	1,194
Daviess	17	10	129	2	41	16	108	215	48	8	3	1	177	37	858
Gibson	11	12	33	0	59	19	74	54	5	8	18	--	5	52	420
Greene	104	34	71	2	212	120	198	431	184	3	68	2	1,147	93	2,721
Knox	0	34	2	4	1	88	18	140	6	1	1	--	265	46	751
Martin	54	23	8	3	354	263	47	464	446	--	37	6	806	31	2,728
Parke	100	129	--	7	121	184	6	282	281	--	69	--	543	114	2,032
P ke	20	3	99	1	23	20	20	110	12	33	27	1	39	50	476
Posey	6	1	--	0	17	3	8	96	40	13	9	1	15	11	254
Putnam	48	146	--	2	285	184	37	188	201	--	2	1	458	56	1,763
Sullivan	65	113	6	18	221	25	49	382	49	--	194	2	162	136	1,658
Vanderburgh	0	--	90	0	1	1	16	12	1	4	1	--	15	1	156
Vermillion	5	5	--	--	21	4	--	125	20	--	1	--	33	8	232
Vigo	50	53	19	6	52	61	147	166	41	--	29	--	47	48	788
Unit total	517	601	458	49	1,456	1,083	856	3,077	1,395	73	498	14	3,951	697	16,031

(Table 11 continued on the next page)

Table 11.—continued

Forest Inventory Unit and county	Black cherry	Black walnut	Cotton-wood	Elm	Hickory	Hard maple	Soft maple	Red oak group	White oak group	Sweet-gum	Syca-more	Tupelo/ gum	Yellow-poplar	Other hardwoods	Total hardwoods
Northern Unit															
Adams	47	9	0	1	17	2	--	30	57	5	2	--	2	0	176
Allen	21	122	0	10	81	176	65	280	317	5	0	--	4	9	1,648
Bartholomew	3	3	--	1	20	31	16	120	21	16	9	--	133	2	414
Blackford	0	9	2	0	1	1	0	5	5	--	--	--	--	--	29
Boone	5	3	--	4	8	4	0	9	21	12	--	--	--	2	103
Carroll	9	19	37	--	17	18	41	51	65	--	--	0	1	--	282
Cass	13	9	0	0	9	34	2	110	68	3	1	--	--	--	276
Clinton	--	1	27	--	4	4	--	4	4	--	8	--	12	3	78
De Kalb	11	34	0	11	11	34	124	31	29	5	62	--	8	1	444
Decatur	1	12	1	2	20	10	17	111	84	3	35	--	138	2	447
Delaware	11	3	0	0	1	11	--	2	1	--	--	--	2	3	37
Elkhart	106	62	75	26	42	25	62	47	5	5	15	--	42	11	645
Fountain	29	35	52	4	11	47	22	55	10	--	17	--	10	5	318
Fulton	18	8	--	1	10	11	2	55	16	--	--	--	6	0	148
Grant	3	36	6	0	29	15	1	6	56	--	--	--	2	--	194
Hamilton	7	7	--	2	33	1	--	--	--	--	8	--	--	2	80
Hancock	3	25	--	1	5	18	2	10	4	--	--	--	2	--	85
Hendricks	34	11	16	1	1	--	0	0	--	--	--	--	--	9	87
Henry	5	9	--	0	1	1	1	6	13	--	8	--	6	--	52
Howard	8	10	2	0	3	16	1	11	6	--	7	--	1	--	78
Huntington	8	25	16	1	37	18	11	2	7	--	18	--	3	1	295
Jasper	13	1	--	1	6	--	30	20	48	--	--	--	--	--	119
Jay	1	6	1	0	33	22	24	36	68	--	--	--	--	--	251
Johnson	20	33	--	1	48	34	2	22	8	--	9	--	4	4	283
Kosciusko	52	41	167	21	28	97	113	110	155	12	77	0	19	26	1,238
La Grange	47	43	41	12	35	42	55	30	78	5	32	--	69	15	559
La Porte	107	20	--	0	3	0	31	113	2	--	--	--	29	0	305
Lake	7	1	--	2	2	--	--	1	48	--	--	--	--	--	62
Madison	8	1	--	0	1	2	3	8	0	--	--	0	--	2	67
Marion	0	11	--	2	4	5	2	0	0	--	13	--	22	7	89
Marshall	73	32	75	3	16	41	60	105	34	7	7	--	14	7	506
Miami	14	48	16	2	3	55	14	62	34	--	6	0	16	2	333
Montgomery	16	85	2	2	24	28	0	32	15	--	6	--	31	9	284
Newton	6	1	--	0	2	--	8	25	31	--	--	--	--	--	72
Noble	104	51	1	16	29	83	85	113	233	5	0	--	2	22	807

County													Total
Porter	7	0	82	2	8	20	8	38	64	--	--	--	9	241
Pulaski	4	10	125	--	2	--	61	194	190	--	--	--	--	587
Randolph	4	4	--	0	9	28	--	27	76	--	--	--	2	166
Rush	3	9	5	0	7	15	3	4	7	--	18	--	4	107
Shelby	0	2	51	0	--	15	1	--	22	--	9	0	--	121
St. Joseph	76	11	--	7	21	12	62	347	58	1	6	--	24	667
Starke	1	4	2	--	5	2	30	85	33	10	--	--	--	171
Steuben	54	83	58	19	43	29	23	130	139	5	57	--	142	883
Tippecanoe	0	29	--	1	16	--	2	42	5	--	--	--	2	115
Tipton	--	0	8	--	--	--	2	--	--	--	--	--	--	12
Wabash	18	19	0	3	15	38	9	70	19	--	2	--	1	276
Warren	9	12	--	2	1	3	--	12	75	--	24	--	57	204
Wayne	2	6	--	0	9	4	0	11	3	--	2	--	3	45
Wells	0	27	--	1	6	13	2	8	126	--	4	--	1	224
White	4	4	26	1	5	0	15	79	25	--	--	--	1	171
Whitley	28	31	76	14	46	110	4	19	42	5	17	0	9	472
Unit total	1,018	1,072	970	175	790	1,175	1,021	2,687	2,429	103	479	1	837	15,354
Upland Flats Unit														
Dearborn	21	35	--	3	42	16	4	139	133	--	8	--	2	468
Fayette	37	9	--	1	9	15	2	11	26	--	17	--	67	270
Franklin	18	23	16	3	58	28	12	179	126	4	39	--	109	683
Jefferson	13	68	--	3	45	44	63	255	50	83	28	0	189	951
Jennings	40	21	0	1	107	57	68	218	379	40	49	--	573	1,742
Ohio	5	1	--	0	0	2	--	14	6	--	--	--	8	73
Ripley	41	18	--	2	56	101	48	93	208	110	47	--	136	1,006
Switzerland	1	25	--	2	25	2	6	2	21	--	8	--	1	114
Union	27	6	1	1	32	11	--	8	5	--	21	--	1	130
Unit total	203	206	17	16	375	277	203	917	955	238	217	0	1,086	5,437
State total	2,867	2,756	1,606	300	5,486	5,731	3,029	14,572	12,727	601	1,913	40	13,623	74,335

All table cells without observations are indicated by -- . Table value of 0 indicates the volume rounds to less than 1 thousand cubic feet. Columns and rows may not add to their totals due to rounding.

Table 12a.—Sawtimber removals from timberland for industrial roundwood, in thousand board feet, International ¼-inch rule, by Forest Inventory Unit, county, and species group, Indiana, 2008

Forest Inventory Unit and county	All species	Softwoods						Hardwoods					
		Eastern redcedar	Loblolly/ shortleaf pine	Red pine	White pine	Other pine	Total softwoods	Ash	Aspen/ balsam poplar	Bass-wood	Beech	White birch	Other birch
Knobs Unit													
Brown	20,572	--	11	--	--	--	11	392	3	7	277	1	--
Clark	7,270	7	--	--	3	201	211	838	--	--	305	--	--
Crawford	12,177	12	34	--	--	37	83	217	--	--	28	--	--
Dubois	11,101	3	11	--	29	--	41	790	--	--	77	--	--
Floyd	3,248	--	--	--	--	52	55	260	--	--	2	--	--
Harrison	9,062	66	--	--	--	361	427	811	45	25	78	--	--
Jackson	17,205	7	--	0	696	472	1,174	1,443	42	5	606	1	--
Lawrence	17,944	2	14	--	569	--	585	543	103	--	352	--	--
Monroe	22,325	10	1	--	399	--	411	1,029	3	122	634	--	--
Morgan	10,058	--	--	--	--	--	--	1,073	3	63	327	--	--
Orange	17,682	22	31	--	421	86	561	549	11	0	241	--	--
Owen	11,658	2	--	--	--	15	17	706	5	58	319	--	--
Perry	9,584	17	88	--	140	3	249	190	--	--	146	--	--
Scott	3,227	36	--	--	--	382	417	18	--	--	92	--	--
Spencer	3,674	2	--	--	--	--	2	367	--	--	81	--	--
Warrick	4,237	--	10	--	--	--	10	227	--	--	74	--	--
Washington	24,233	24	--	--	--	1,024	1,048	1,227	--	2	392	--	--
Unit total	**205,256**	**209**	**201**	**0**	**2,257**	**2,633**	**5,300**	**10,681**	**213**	**283**	**4,028**	**2**	**--**
Lower Wabash Unit													
Clay	6,390	--	--	--	38	13	51	372	--	--	23	1	--
Daviess	4,606	--	--	--	--	--	--	236	--	--	3	--	--
Gibson	2,228	--	--	--	--	--	--	358	--	--	5	--	--
Greene	14,649	--	5	--	100	31	136	145	--	22	104	3	--
Knox	3,651	--	--	--	--	--	--	688	--	--	6	--	--
Martin	14,573	2	--	--	--	10	12	647	--	4	314	1	0
Parke	10,950	--	--	--	--	--	--	621	--	88	325	5	--
Pike	3,494	2	22	--	786	95	905	86	--	--	2	--	--
Posey	1,211	--	--	--	--	--	--	149	--	--	--	--	--
Putnam	9,513	--	--	--	--	--	--	679	--	62	64	--	--
Sullivan	7,784	--	--	--	17	5	22	1,080	--	9	2	0	6
Vanderburgh	827	--	--	--	--	--	--	72	--	--	--	--	--
Vermillion	1,254	--	--	--	--	--	--	23	2	24	--	--	--
Vigo	4,165	--	--	--	--	--	--	253	--	109	--	--	--
Unit total	**85,296**	**3**	**26**	**--**	**942**	**154**	**1,126**	**5,409**	**2**	**319**	**847**	**10**	**6**

Forest Inventory Unit and county	All species	Eastern redcedar	Loblolly/ shortleaf pine	Red pine	White pine	Other pine	Total softwoods	Ash	Aspen/ balsam poplar	Bass- wood	Beech	White birch	Other birch
Northern Unit													
Adams	1,015	--	--	--	--	--	--	26	--	--	--	--	--
Allen	8,830	--	--	--	--	--	--	445	--	1,952	576	--	--
Bartholomew	2,189	--	--	--	--	--	--	81	5	--	122	--	--
Blackford	169	--	--	--	--	--	--	26	0	--	--	--	--
Boone	548	--	--	--	--	--	--	185	--	--	6	--	--
Carroll	1,520	--	--	--	--	--	--	53	--	46	23	--	--
Cass	1,464	--	--	--	--	--	--	136	--	12	--	--	--
Clinton	428	--	--	--	--	--	--	21	--	--	23	--	--
De Kalb	2,377	--	--	--	--	--	--	277	--	156	3	--	--
Decatur	2,382	--	--	--	--	--	--	45	--	--	14	--	--
Delaware	197	--	--	--	--	--	--	6	--	--	--	--	--
Elkhart	3,545	--	--	31	--	--	31	506	0	47	97	--	--
Fountain	1,756	--	--	--	--	--	--	105	--	4	3	--	--
Fulton	786	--	--	--	--	--	--	65	--	41	--	--	--
Grant	1,064	--	--	--	--	--	--	204	0	4	--	--	--
Hamilton	433	--	--	--	--	--	--	111	--	--	--	--	--
Hancock	468	--	--	--	--	--	--	78	--	--	--	--	--
Hendricks	499	--	--	--	--	--	--	70	--	2	--	--	--
Henry	291	--	--	--	--	--	--	7	--	9	--	--	--
Howard	423	--	--	--	--	--	--	63	--	8	--	--	--
Huntington	1,594	--	--	--	--	--	--	621	0	92	73	--	--
Jasper	626	--	--	--	--	--	--	--	--	--	--	--	--
Jay	1,327	--	--	--	--	--	--	293	0	16	4	--	--
Johnson	1,541	--	--	--	--	--	--	458	--	--	47	--	--
Kosciusko	6,681	--	--	--	--	--	--	1,569	0	90	49	--	--
La Grange	3,121	--	--	10	72	--	82	188	14	88	3	--	--
La Porte	1,651	--	--	--	--	--	--	3	--	--	--	--	--
Lake	336	--	--	--	--	--	--	15	3	--	--	--	--
Madison	357	--	--	--	--	--	--	198	--	14	--	--	--
Marion	479	--	--	--	--	--	--	131	--	2	--	--	--
Marshall	2,745	--	--	--	--	--	--	125	--	48	4	--	--
Miami	1,813	--	--	--	--	--	--	285	0	35	3	--	--
Montgomery	1,606	--	--	--	--	--	--	155	14	8	6	--	--
Newton	388	--	--	--	--	--	--	--	--	--	--	--	--
Noble	4,304	--	--	--	--	--	--	293	--	11	26	--	--
Porter	1,321	--	--	--	--	--	--	16	2	--	--	--	--
Pulaski	3,183	--	--	--	--	--	--	--	--	--	--	--	--

(Table 12 continued on the next page)

Table 12a.—continued

County / Unit												
Randolph	909	—	—	—	—	—	72	—	—	5	—	—	—
Rush	586	—	—	—	—	—	156	—	—	—	—	—	—
Shelby	686	—	—	—	—	—	98	—	—	—	—	—	—
St. Joseph	3,541	—	—	—	—	—	97	—	25	—	—	—	—
Starke	917	—	—	—	—	—	—	—	—	—	—	—	—
Steuben	4,803	—	—	—	—	—	430	6	37	3	—	—	—
Tippecanoe	642	—	—	—	—	—	69	—	3	—	—	—	—
Tipton	54	—	—	—	—	—	5	—	—	—	—	—	—
Wabash	1,496	—	—	—	2	2	371	—	55	8	—	—	—
Warren	1,089	—	—	—	—	—	33	—	18	—	—	—	—
Wayne	251	—	—	—	—	—	22	—	—	—	—	—	—
Wells	1,207	—	—	—	—	—	183	—	2	—	—	—	—
White	930	—	—	—	—	—	32	—	29	—	—	—	—
Whitley	2,775	—	—	—	217	217	157	33	98	—	—	—	—
Unit total	**83,340**	**389**	**177**	**41**	**291**	**333**	**8,587**	**75**	**2,949**	**1,096**	**—**	**—**	**—**
Upland Flats Unit												
Dearborn	2,505	1	—	—	—	1	283	—	14	—	—	—	—
Fayette	1,434	0	—	—	—	0	353	—	—	0	—	—	—
Franklin	3,685	—	—	—	—	—	279	—	—	36	—	—	—
Jefferson	5,195	71	—	13	13	97	229	—	300	23	—	—	—
Jennings	9,461	34	157	—	—	191	496	—	92	377	—	—	—
Ohio	364	0	—	—	—	0	165	—	—	0	—	—	—
Ripley	5,393	35	—	—	—	35	357	—	128	196	—	—	—
Switzerland	664	35	—	—	—	35	86	—	—	—	—	—	—
Union	720	0	—	—	—	0	80	—	—	9	—	—	—
Unit total	**29,421**	**177**	**170**	**13**	**13**	**360**	**2,327**	**—**	**534**	**641**	**0**	**0**	**—**
State total	**403,313**	**3,660**	**389**	**228**	**2,800**	**7,119**	**27,004**	**290**	**4,084**	**6,612**	**0**	**12**	**6**

Forest Inventory Unit and county	Black cherry	Black walnut	Cotton-wood	Elm	Hickory	Hard maple	Soft maple	Red oak group	White oak group	Sweet-gum	Syca-more	Tupelo/gum	Yellow-poplar	Other hardwoods	Total hardwoods
Knobs Unit															
Brown	559	225	--	34	1,811	1,341	699	8,218	5,463	3	338	16	877	301	20,561
Clark	93	310	--	0	632	344	109	924	1,164	165	90	--	2,029	55	7,059
Crawford	428	129	--	24	1,369	939	90	3,019	4,057	--	324	9	1,287	175	12,094
Dubois	417	496	--	16	803	804	572	1,763	2,481	143	172	12	1,868	646	11,061
Floyd	53	65	--	--	119	235	46	534	1,722	2	--	2	74	78	3,193
Harrison	778	238	8	37	498	1,221	143	2,205	1,059	--	34	6	1,164	286	8,635
Jackson	445	289	64	16	620	1,453	786	2,341	2,261	281	875	12	4,277	213	16,031
Lawrence	885	435	28	38	788	1,147	282	4,042	2,051	--	736	7	5,465	460	17,360
Monroe	873	1,495	--	36	2,483	1,255	379	3,791	4,395	33	156	3	4,806	420	21,913
Morgan	115	257	587	8	707	1,100	365	2,109	621	--	121	6	2,374	220	10,058
Orange	267	543	--	23	808	1,678	139	4,269	3,199	48	283	8	4,292	762	17,121
Owen	51	140	20	16	829	1,216	292	1,370	918	12	41	9	5,443	197	11,641
Perry	110	91	--	25	1,078	1,071	308	2,008	2,984	65	59	15	1,034	150	9,336
Scott	85	167	--	0	160	557	27	42	900	10	10	14	669	60	2,810
Spencer	255	98	--	3	622	176	296	663	589	123	121	--	45	234	3,672
Warrick	31	49	243	7	379	139	272	1,747	462	104	200	6	174	115	4,227
Washington	701	514	--	40	1,576	1,998	73	2,791	7,844	--	254	6	5,557	210	23,185
Unit total	6,146	5,539	951	322	15,282	16,675	4,877	41,839	42,170	989	3,813	131	41,434	4,582	199,956
Lower Wabash Unit															
Clay	196	234	--	13	264	487	666	2,179	334	18	208	--	1,276	66	6,339
Daviess	91	65	766	11	218	81	553	1,128	254	43	15	3	942	196	4,606
Gibson	62	80	198	3	314	97	378	283	28	33	88	--	25	277	2,228
Greene	556	217	421	14	1,124	620	1,015	2,269	978	14	363	12	6,139	497	14,514
Knox	0	184	13	16	5	414	85	679	25	6	8	--	1,302	221	3,651
Martin	322	148	50	18	1,881	1,363	240	2,481	2,383	--	194	32	4,315	167	14,561
Parke	544	823	--	39	646	968	30	1,495	1,505	--	366	--	2,893	606	10,950
Pike	107	22	589	8	120	105	102	583	64	175	141	6	208	266	2,589
Posey	33	8	--	2	90	18	41	478	189	41	21	5	78	60	1,211
Putnam	258	930	--	9	1,509	954	187	996	1,089	--	10	8	2,458	299	9,513
Sullivan	305	579	31	76	1,035	112	222	1,801	228	--	874	7	769	624	7,762
Vanderburgh	2	--	493	1	6	6	77	62	2	23	6	--	74	3	827
Vermillion	28	31	--	--	112	25	--	676	108	--	3	--	176	44	1,254
Vigo	267	335	112	31	272	311	745	866	213	--	149	--	247	254	4,165
Unit total	2,774	3,655	2,674	241	7,597	5,563	4,342	15,975	7,403	351	2,447	73	20,904	3,581	84,170

(Table 12 continued on the next page)

Table 12a.—continued

| | | | | | | Hardwoods | | | | | | | | |
Forest Inventory Unit and county	Black cherry	Black walnut	Cotton-wood	Elm	Hickory	Hard maple	Soft maple	Red oak group	White oak group	Sweet-gum	Syca-more	Tupelo/gum	Yellow-poplar	Other hardwoods	Total hardwoods
Northern Unit															
Adams	320	54	1	5	90	9	--	158	305	26	9	--	10	2	1,015
Allen	109	769	2	55	431	906	331	1,478	1,682	26	1	--	23	46	8,830
Bartholomew	17	21	--	4	103	169	81	629	111	84	48	--	705	10	2,189
Blackford	0	54	10	0	7	7	0	27	37	--	--	--	--	--	169
Boone	24	18	--	20	42	20	0	47	111	66	--	--	--	11	548
Carroll	46	121	222	--	92	92	211	270	340	--	--	1	3	--	1,520
Cass	68	55	--	1	47	172	10	579	358	18	3	--	3	--	1,464
Clinton	--	5	158	--	21	20	20	21	21	--	42	--	62	14	428
De Kalb	60	217	1	60	59	176	636	165	165	26	328	--	44	3	2,377
Decatur	5	74	4	11	108	51	88	589	453	14	184	--	732	9	2,382
Delaware	61	20	2	2	6	55	--	11	6	--	--	--	13	16	197
Elkhart	566	389	444	139	221	128	315	245	27	27	80	--	225	58	3,514
Fountain	157	217	309	21	59	242	113	299	54	--	92	--	52	29	1,756
Fulton	95	52	--	4	53	54	12	291	85	--	--	--	33	2	786
Grant	14	228	36	0	154	79	5	33	296	--	--	--	11	--	1,064
Hamilton	36	42	--	11	176	3	--	52	19	--	45	--	--	9	433
Hancock	15	157	--	3	28	93	9	52	19	--	--	--	13	--	468
Hendricks	198	70	96	6	3	--	6	2	--	--	--	--	--	46	499
Henry	27	57	--	0	8	5	1	37	69	--	40	--	29	--	291
Howard	41	61	10	2	17	83	4	58	34	--	36	--	8	--	423
Huntington	41	155	96	4	197	91	56	12	39	--	95	--	14	7	1,594
Jasper	68	9	--	4	32	115	156	107	250	--	--	--	--	--	626
Jay	8	39	5	0	179	193	124	188	356	--	--	--	--	--	1,327
Johnson	107	212	--	5	254	495	11	116	44	--	49	--	23	24	1,541
Kosciusko	274	255	989	112	150	219	580	585	823	62	411	1	102	136	6,681
La Grange	253	268	244	62	190	0	280	162	421	26	170	--	368	82	3,038
La Porte	576	123	--	2	17	--	159	606	12	--	--	--	152	2	1,651
Lake	36	5	--	--	10	10	--	6	261	--	--	--	--	--	336
Madison	44	4	--	0	8	37	17	42	6	--	--	1	13	--	357
Marion	1	68	--	9	23	--	9	0	0	--	69	--	119	11	479
Marshall	388	204	444	15	84	210	306	552	180	38	39	--	74	35	2,745
Miami	73	300	95	13	14	283	72	335	178	--	32	1	85	9	1,813
Montgomery	95	539	15	12	132	142	3	169	78	--	32	--	162	46	1,606
Newton	33	4	--	2	12	--	39	129	170	26	--	--	--	--	388
Noble	556	319	5	87	155	428	434	599	1,233	26	1	--	12	119	4,304
Porter	37	1	484	10	43	105	41	201	334	--	--	--	47	--	1,321
Pulaski	23	62	740	--	12	--	313	1,031	1,000	2	--	--	--	--	3,183

County														Total
Randolph	24	28	--	2	49	149	--	157	409	--	--	--	13	1	909
Rush	20	57	30	0	39	83	16	24	43	--	95	1	21	1	586
Shelby	1	12	305	0	--	91	7	--	126	--	46	--	--	--	686
St. Joseph	416	75	--	35	112	61	316	1,833	304	6	32	--	128	102	3,541
Starke	5	25	12	--	26	12	152	446	189	51	--	--	--	--	917
Steuben	299	521	342	99	229	149	117	682	737	26	301	--	756	70	4,803
Tippecanoe	2	183	--	8	89	--	10	220	27	--	--	--	13	18	642
Tipton	--	1	35	--	--	--	7	--	--	--	--	--	--	6	54
Wabash	97	119	1	14	77	200	48	373	108	--	11	--	3	9	1,494
Warren	47	74	--	9	3	17	--	63	394	--	128	--	301	2	1,089
Wayne	11	39	--	0	47	20	1	66	18	--	13	--	14	--	251
Wells	0	168	--	3	34	68	12	44	664	--	22	--	8	--	1,207
White	20	23	157	3	29	1	79	424	132	--	--	--	3	--	930
Whitley	150	196	452	75	245	565	20	98	222	26	92	1	50	78	2,558
Unit total	5,565	6,771	5,748	929	4,215	6,109	5,230	14,259	12,927	546	2,545	6	4,445	1,007	83,007
Upland Flats Unit															
Dearborn	113	225	--	17	223	83	18	730	707	44	--	--	11	35	2,504
Fayette	210	61	--	4	50	79	8	55	149	91	--	--	353	21	1,434
Franklin	98	155	95	19	310	153	59	960	686	22	205	--	577	32	3,685
Jefferson	72	437	--	14	240	234	326	1,345	275	442	147	1	1,004	11	5,098
Jennings	213	134	1	8	566	304	349	1,155	2,015	214	259	--	3,070	18	9,270
Ohio	29	4	--	3	3	12	--	72	31	--	--	--	43	2	363
Ripley	235	120	--	9	294	532	249	498	1,103	586	250	--	736	62	5,357
Switzerland	6	167	--	8	132	12	33	12	108	--	41	--	6	18	629
Union	147	38	6	4	168	60	--	43	38	--	114	--	7	6	720
Unit total	1,123	1,342	102	86	1,985	1,469	1,042	4,871	5,112	1,264	1,151	1	5,807	204	29,061
State total	15,608	17,307	9,475	1,578	29,078	29,815	15,492	76,943	67,611	3,150	9,955	211	72,589	9,374	396,194

All table cells without observations are indicated by -- . Table value of 0 indicates the volume rounds to less than 1 thousand board feet. Columns and rows may not add to their totals due to rounding.

Table 12b.—Sawtimber removals from timberland for industrial roundwood, in thousand board feet, Doyle rule, by Forest Inventory Unit, county, and species group, Indiana, 2008

Forest Inventory Unit and county	All species	Softwoods						Hardwoods					
		Eastern redcedar	Loblolly/ shortleaf pine	Red pine	White pine	Other pine	Total softwoods	Ash	Aspen/ balsam poplar	Bass-wood	Beech	White birch	Other birch
Knobs Unit													
Brown	14,907	--	8	--	--	--	8	284	2	5	201	1	--
Clark	5,268	5	--	--	2	146	153	607	--	--	221	--	--
Crawford	8,824	9	25	--	--	27	60	157	--	--	20	--	--
Dubois	8,044	--	8	--	21	--	30	572	--	--	56	--	--
Floyd	2,354	2	--	--	--	38	40	188	--	--	1	--	--
Harrison	6,567	48	--	--	--	262	309	588	33	18	57	--	--
Jackson	12,467	5	--	0	504	342	851	1,046	30	4	439	--	--
Lawrence	13,003	1	10	--	412	--	424	393	75	--	255	1	--
Monroe	16,178	7	1	--	289	--	298	746	1	88	459	--	--
Morgan	7,288	--	--	--	--	--	--	778	2	46	237	--	--
Orange	12,813	16	22	--	305	62	407	398	8	0	175	--	--
Owen	8,448	1	--	--	--	11	12	512	4	42	231	--	--
Perry	6,945	12	64	--	101	2	180	138	--	--	106	--	--
Scott	2,338	26	--	--	--	277	302	13	--	--	67	--	--
Spencer	2,662	1	--	--	--	--	1	266	--	--	59	--	--
Warrick	3,070	--	7	--	--	--	7	164	--	--	54	--	--
Washington	17,560	17	--	--	--	742	759	889	--	1	284	--	--
Unit total	148,736	151	146	0	1,636	1,908	3,841	7,740	154	205	2,919	1	--
Lower Wabash Unit													
Clay	4,630	--	--	--	28	9	37	270	--	--	17	1	--
Daviess	3,338	--	--	--	--	--	--	171	--	--	2	--	--
Gibson	1,614	--	--	--	--	--	--	259	--	--	4	--	--
Greene	10,615	--	4	--	72	22	99	105	--	16	75	2	--
Knox	2,646	--	--	--	--	--	--	499	--	--	4	--	--
Martin	10,560	1	--	--	--	7	9	469	--	3	228	1	0
Parke	7,935	--	--	--	--	--	--	450	--	64	236	--	--
Pike	2,532	1	16	--	570	69	656	62	--	--	1	4	--
Posey	878	--	--	--	--	--	--	108	--	--	--	--	--
Putnam	6,893	--	--	--	--	--	--	492	--	45	46	--	--
Sullivan	5,641	--	--	--	12	4	16	783	--	7	1	0	4
Vanderburgh	599	--	--	--	--	--	--	52	--	--	--	--	--
Vermillion	909	--	--	--	--	--	--	17	1	17	--	--	--
Vigo	3,018	--	--	--	--	--	--	183	--	79	--	--	--
Unit total	61,809	2	19	--	683	112	816	3,920	1	231	614	7	4

60

Forest Inventory Unit and county	All species	Eastern redcedar	Loblolly/ shortleaf pine	Red pine	White pine	Other pine	Total softwoods	Ash	Aspen/ balsam poplar	Bass- wood	Beech	White birch	Other birch
Northern Unit													
Adams	736	--	--	--	--	--	--	19	--	--	--	--	--
Allen	6,399	--	--	--	--	--	--	322	--	1,414	417	--	--
Bartholomew	1,586	--	--	--	--	--	--	59	4	--	88	--	--
Blackford	122	--	--	--	--	--	--	19	0	--	--	--	--
Boone	397	--	--	--	--	--	--	134	--	--	4	--	--
Carroll	1,101	--	--	--	--	--	--	38	--	33	17	--	--
Cass	1,061	--	--	--	--	--	--	99	--	9	--	--	--
Clinton	310	--	--	--	--	--	--	15	--	--	17	--	--
De Kalb	1,722	--	--	--	--	--	--	201	--	113	2	--	--
Decatur	1,726	--	--	--	--	--	--	33	--	--	10	--	--
Delaware	143	--	--	--	--	--	--	4	--	--	--	--	--
Elkhart	2,569	--	--	22	--	--	22	367	0	34	70	--	--
Fountain	1,272	--	--	--	--	--	--	76	--	3	2	--	--
Fulton	570	--	--	--	--	--	--	47	--	30	--	--	--
Grant	771	--	--	--	--	--	--	148	0	3	--	--	--
Hamilton	314	--	--	--	--	--	--	80	--	--	--	--	--
Hancock	339	--	--	--	--	--	--	57	--	--	--	--	--
Hendricks	362	--	--	--	--	--	--	51	--	1	--	--	--
Henry	211	--	--	--	--	--	--	5	--	7	--	--	--
Howard	307	--	--	--	--	--	--	46	--	6	--	--	--
Huntington	1,155	--	--	--	--	--	--	450	0	67	53	--	--
Jasper	454	--	--	--	--	--	--	--	--	--	--	--	--
Jay	962	--	--	--	--	--	--	212	0	12	3	--	--
Johnson	1,117	--	--	--	--	--	--	332	--	--	34	--	--
Kosciusko	4,841	--	--	--	--	--	--	1,137	0	65	36	--	--
La Grange	2,262	--	--	7	52	--	59	136	10	64	2	--	--
La Porte	1,196	--	--	--	--	--	--	2	--	--	--	--	--
Lake	243	--	--	--	--	--	--	11	2	--	--	--	--
Madison	259	--	--	--	--	--	--	143	--	10	--	--	--
Marion	347	--	--	--	--	--	--	95	--	1	--	--	--
Marshall	1,989	--	--	--	--	--	--	91	--	35	3	--	--
Miami	1,314	--	--	--	--	--	--	207	0	25	2	--	--
Montgomery	1,164	--	--	--	--	--	--	112	10	6	4	--	--

(Table 12 continued on the next page)

Table 12b.—continued

Newton	281	—	—	—	—	—	—	—	—	—
Noble	3,119	—	—	—	—	—	212	—	8	19
Porter	957	—	—	—	—	—	12	1	—	—
Pulaski	2,307	—	—	—	—	—	—	—	—	—
Randolph	659	—	—	—	—	—	52	—	—	4
Rush	425	—	—	—	—	—	113	—	—	—
Shelby	497	—	—	—	—	—	71	—	—	—
St. Joseph	2,566	—	—	—	—	—	70	—	18	—
Starke	664	—	—	—	—	—	—	—	—	—
Steuben	3,480	—	—	—	—	—	312	4	27	2
Tippecanoe	465	—	—	—	—	—	50	—	2	—
Tipton	39	—	—	—	—	—	4	—	—	—
Wabash	1,084	—	—	1	—	1	269	—	40	6
Warren	789	—	—	—	—	—	24	—	13	—
Wayne	182	—	—	—	—	—	16	—	—	—
Wells	875	—	—	—	—	—	133	—	1	—
White	674	—	—	—	—	—	23	—	21	—
Whitley	2,011	—	157	157	—	157	114	24	71	—
Unit total	**60,391**	—	30	211	30	241	6,222	54	2,137	794
Upland Flats Unit										
Dearborn	1,815	1	—	—	—	1	205	—	10	—
Fayette	1,039	0	—	—	—	0	256	—	—	0
Franklin	2,670	—	—	—	—	—	202	—	—	26
Jefferson	3,764	51	—	9	—	70	166	—	217	17
Jennings	6,856	25	—	114	9	138	359	—	67	273
Ohio	264	0	—	—	—	0	120	—	—	0
Ripley	3,908	25	—	—	—	25	259	—	93	142
Switzerland	481	25	—	—	—	25	62	—	—	—
Union	522	0	—	—	—	0	58	—	—	7
Unit total	**21,320**	128	—	123	9	261	1,686	—	387	464
State total	**292,256**	282	165	2,652	2,029	5,159	19,568	210	2,959	4,791

Forest Inventory Unit and county	Black cherry	Black walnut	Cotton-wood	Elm	Hickory	Hard maple	Soft maple	Hardwoods Red oak group	White oak group	Sweet-gum	Syca-more	Tupelo/ gum	Yellow-poplar	Other hardwoods	Total hardwoods
Knobs Unit															
Brown	405	163	--	25	1,312	972	507	5,955	3,959	2	245	12	636	218	14,899
Clark	67	225	--	0	458	249	79	670	843	120	65	--	1,470	40	5,115
Crawford	310	93	--	17	992	680	65	2,188	2,940	--	235	7	933	127	8,764
Dubois	302	359	--	12	582	583	414	1,278	1,798	104	125	9	1,354	468	8,015
Floyd	38	47	--	--	86	170	33	387	1,248	1	--	1	54	57	2,314
Harrison	564	172	6	27	361	885	104	1,598	767	--	25	4	843	207	6,257
Jackson	322	209	46	12	449	1,053	570	1,696	1,638	204	634	9	3,099	154	11,617
Lawrence	641	315	20	28	571	831	204	2,929	1,486	--	533	5	3,960	333	12,580
Monroe	633	1,083	--	26	1,799	909	275	2,747	3,185	24	113	2	3,483	304	15,879
Morgan	83	186	425	6	512	797	264	1,528	450	--	88	4	1,720	159	7,288
Orange	193	393	--	17	586	1,216	101	3,093	2,318	35	205	6	3,110	552	12,407
Owen	37	101	14	12	601	881	212	993	665	9	30	7	3,944	143	8,436
Perry	80	66	--	18	781	776	223	1,455	2,162	47	43	11	749	109	6,765
Scott	62	121	--	0	116	404	20	30	652	7	7	10	485	43	2,036
Spencer	185	71	--	2	451	128	214	480	427	89	88	--	33	170	2,661
Warrick	22	36	176	5	275	101	197	1,266	335	75	145	4	126	83	3,063
Washington	508	372	--	29	1,142	1,448	53	2,022	5,684	--	184	4	4,027	152	16,801
Unit total	4,454	4,014	689	233	11,074	12,083	3,534	30,318	30,558	717	2,763	95	30,025	3,320	144,896
Lower Wabash Unit															
Clay	142	170	--	9	191	353	483	1,579	242	13	151	--	925	48	4,593
Daviess	66	47	555	8	158	59	401	817	184	31	11	2	683	142	3,338
Gibson	45	58	143	2	228	70	274	205	20	24	64	--	18	201	1,614
Greene	403	157	305	10	814	449	736	1,644	709	10	263	9	4,449	360	10,517
Knox	0	133	9	12	4	300	62	492	18	4	6	--	943	160	2,646
Martin	233	107	36	13	1,363	988	174	1,798	1,727	--	141	23	3,127	121	10,551
Parke	394	596	--	28	468	701	22	1,083	1,091	--	265	--	2,096	439	7,935
P ke	78	16	427	6	87	76	74	422	46	127	102	4	151	193	1,876
Posey	24	6	--	1	65	13	30	346	137	30	15	4	57	43	878
Putnam	187	674	--	7	1,093	691	136	722	789	--	7	6	1,781	217	6,893
Sullivan	221	420	22	55	750	81	161	1,305	165	--	633	5	557	452	5,625
Vanderburgh	1	--	357	1	4	4	56	45	1	17	4	--	54	2	599
Vermillion	20	22	--	--	81	18	--	490	78	--	2	--	128	32	909
Vigo	193	243	81	22	197	225	540	628	154	--	108	--	179	184	3,018
Unit total	2,010	2,649	1,938	175	5,505	4,031	3,146	11,576	5,364	254	1,773	53	15,148	2,595	60,993

(Table 12 continued on the next page)

Table 12b.—continued

Forest Inventory Unit and county	Black cherry	Black walnut	Cotton-wood	Elm	Hickory	Hard maple	Soft maple	Hardwoods		Sweet-gum	Syca-more	Tupelo/gum	Yellow-poplar	Other hardwoods	Total hardwoods
								Red oak group	White oak group						
Northern Unit															
Adams	232	39	1	4	65	7	--	114	221	19	7	--	7	1	736
Allen	79	557	1	40	312	657	240	1,071	1,219	19	1	--	17	33	6,399
Bartholomew	12	15	--	3	75	122	59	456	80	61	35	--	511	7	1,586
Blackford	0	39	7	5	5	5	1	20	27	--	--	--	--	--	122
Boone	17	13	--	14	30	14	0	34	80	48	--	--	--	8	397
Carroll	33	88	161	--	67	67	153	196	246	--	--	1	2	--	1,101
Cass	49	40	--	1	34	125	7	420	259	13	2	--	2	--	1,061
Clinton	--	4	114	--	15	14	14	15	15	--	30	--	45	10	310
De Kalb	43	157	1	43	43	128	461	120	120	19	238	--	32	2	1,722
Decatur	4	54	3	8	78	37	64	427	328	10	133	--	530	7	1,726
Delaware	44	14	1	1	4	40	--	8	4	--	--	--	9	12	143
E khart	410	282	322	101	160	93	228	178	20	20	58	--	163	42	2,546
Fountain	114	157	224	15	43	175	82	217	39	--	67	--	38	21	1,272
Fulton	69	38	--	38	38	39	9	211	62	--	--	--	24	1	570
Grant	10	165	26	0	112	57	4	24	214	--	--	--	8	--	771
Hamilton	26	30	--	8	128	2	--	38	14	--	33	--	7	7	314
Hancock	11	114	--	2	20	67	7	38	14	--	--	--	9	--	339
Hendricks	143	51	70	4	2	--	4	1	--	--	--	--	--	33	362
Henry	20	41	--	0	6	4	1	27	50	--	29	--	21	--	211
Howard	30	44	7	1	12	60	3	42	25	--	26	--	6	--	307
Huntington	30	112	70	3	143	66	41	9	28	--	69	--	10	5	1,155
Jasper	49	7	--	3	23	--	113	78	181	--	--	--	--	--	454
Jay	6	28	4	0	130	83	90	136	258	--	--	--	--	--	962
Johnson	78	154	--	4	184	140	8	84	32	--	36	--	17	17	1,117
Kosciusko	199	185	717	81	109	359	420	424	596	45	298	1	74	99	4,841
La Grange	183	194	177	45	138	159	203	117	305	19	123	--	267	59	2,201
La Porte	417	89	--	1	12	0	115	439	9	--	--	--	110	1	1,196
Lake	26	4	--	--	7	--	--	4	189	--	--	--	--	--	243
Madison	32	3	--	0	6	7	12	30	4	--	--	1	9	--	259
Marion	1	49	--	7	17	27	7	0	0	--	--	--	86	8	347
Marshall	281	148	322	11	61	152	222	400	130	28	50	--	54	25	1,989
Miami	53	217	69	9	10	205	52	243	129	--	28	1	62	7	1,314
Montgomery	69	391	11	9	96	103	2	122	57	--	23	--	117	33	1,164

County															Total
Newton	24	3	--	1	9	--	28	93	123	--	--	--	--	--	281
Noble	403	231	4	63	112	310	314	434	893	19	--	--	9	86	3,119
Porter	27	1	351	7	31	76	30	146	242	--	--	--	34	--	957
Pulaski	17	45	536	--	9	--	227	747	725	1	--	--	--	--	2,307
Randolph	17	20	--	1	36	108	--	114	296	--	--	--	9	1	659
Rush	14	41	22	0	28	60	12	17	31	69	--	1	15	1	425
Shelby	1	9	--	0	--	66	5	--	91	33	--	--	33	--	497
St. Joseph	301	54	221	25	81	44	229	1,328	220	23	4	--	93	74	2,566
Starke	4	18	--	--	19	9	110	323	137	37	--	--	--	--	664
Steuben	217	378	248	72	166	108	85	494	534	218	--	19	548	51	3,480
Tippecanoe	1	133	--	6	64	--	7	159	20	--	--	--	9	13	465
Tipton	--	--	25	--	--	--	5	--	--	--	--	--	--	4	39
Wabash	70	86	1	10	56	145	35	270	78	8	--	--	2	7	1,083
Warren	34	54	--	7	2	12	--	46	286	93	--	1	218	1	789
Wayne	8	28	--	0	34	14	1	48	13	9	--	--	10	--	182
Wells	0	122	--	2	25	49	9	32	481	16	--	--	6	--	875
White	14	17	114	2	21	1	57	307	96	--	--	--	2	--	674
Whitley	109	142	328	54	178	409	14	71	161	67	--	19	36	57	1,854
Unit total	4,033	4,907	4,165	673	3,054	4,427	3,790	10,333	9,367	396	4	1,844	3,221	730	60,150
Upland Flats Unit															
Dearborn	82	163	--	12	162	60	13	529	512	32	--	--	8	25	1,814
Fayette	152	44	--	3	36	57	6	40	108	66	--	--	256	15	1,039
Franklin	71	112	69	14	225	111	43	696	497	149	--	16	418	23	2,670
Jefferson	52	317	--	10	174	170	236	975	199	107	1	320	728	8	3,694
Jennings	154	97	1	6	410	220	253	837	1,460	188	--	155	2,225	13	6,717
Ohio	21	3	--	2	2	9	--	52	22	31	--	--	31	1	263
Ripley	170	87	--	7	213	386	180	361	799	181	--	425	533	45	3,882
Switzerland	4	121	--	6	96	9	24	9	78	30	--	--	4	13	456
Union	107	28	4	3	122	43	--	31	28	83	--	--	5	4	522
Unit total	814	972	74	62	1,438	1,064	755	3,530	3,704	916	1	834	4,208	148	21,059
State total	11,310	12,541	6,866	1,143	21,071	21,605	11,226	55,756	48,993	2,283	153	7,214	52,601	6,793	287,097

All table cells without observations are indicated by -- . Table value of 0 indicates the volume rounds to less than 1 thousand board feet. Columns and rows may not add to their totals due to rounding.

Table 13.—Harvest residue generated by industrial roundwood harvesting, in thousand cubic feet, by Forest Inventory Unit, county, and species group, Indiana, 2008

Forest Inventory Unit and county	All species	Softwoods						Hardwoods					
		Eastern redcedar	Loblolly/ shortleaf pine	Red pine	White pine	Other pine	Total softwoods	Ash	Aspen/ balsam poplar	Bass-wood	Beech	White birch	Other birch
Knobs Unit													
Brown	2,594	--	2	--	--	--	2	55	0	1	37	0	--
Clark	927	1	--	--	1	45	47	118	--	--	43	--	--
Crawford	1,521	1	6	--	--	9	16	31	--	--	4	--	--
Dubois	1,263	--	3	--	7	--	10	104	--	--	9	--	--
Floyd	357	0	--	--	--	12	12	37	--	--	0	--	--
Harrison	1,212	8	--	--	--	82	90	114	6	4	11	--	--
Jackson	2,413	1	--	0	163	111	275	204	6	1	86	0	--
Lawrence	2,365	0	3	--	134	--	137	76	15	--	47	--	--
Monroe	2,807	1	0	--	94	--	95	145	0	17	87	--	--
Morgan	1,291	--	--	--	--	--	--	151	0	9	44	--	--
Orange	2,270	3	6	--	96	20	125	77	1	0	31	--	--
Owen	1,548	0	--	--	--	4	4	100	1	8	45	--	--
Perry	1,244	2	17	--	32	1	52	27	--	--	20	--	--
Scott	423	4	--	--	--	90	94	3	--	--	13	--	--
Spencer	479	0	--	--	--	--	0	52	--	--	12	--	--
Warrick	548	--	2	--	--	--	2	32	--	--	10	--	--
Washington	2,886	3	--	--	--	241	244	173	--	0	55	--	--
Unit total	26,149	26	39	0	527	613	1,205	1,497	30	40	557	0	--
Lower Wabash Unit													
Clay	843	--	--	--	9	3	12	53	--	--	3	0	--
Daviess	600	--	--	--	--	--	--	33	--	--	0	--	--
Gibson	291	--	--	--	--	--	--	51	--	--	1	--	--
Greene	1,975	--	1	--	23	7	32	20	--	3	15	0	--
Knox	325	--	--	--	--	--	--	61	--	--	1	--	--
Martin	1,887	0	--	--	--	2	3	91	--	1	45	0	0
Parke	1,389	--	4	--	--	--	--	87	--	13	46	--	--
Pike	537	0	--	--	179	21	205	12	--	--	0	0	--
Posey	157	--	--	--	--	--	--	19	--	--	--	--	--
Putnam	1,182	--	--	--	--	--	--	95	--	9	9	--	--
Sullivan	539	--	--	--	4	1	5	74	--	1	0	0	0
Vanderburgh	85	--	--	--	--	--	--	9	--	--	--	--	--
Vermillion	154	--	--	--	--	--	--	3	0	3	--	--	--
Vigo	511	--	--	--	--	--	--	34	--	14	--	--	--
Unit total	10,476	0	5	--	216	35	256	644	0	43	120	0	0

Forest Inventory Unit and county	All species	Softwoods						Hardwoods					
		Eastern redcedar	Loblolly/ shortleaf pine	Red pine	White pine	Other pine	Total softwoods	Ash	Aspen/ balsam poplar	Bass- wood	Beech	White birch	Other birch
Northern Unit													
Adams	95	--	--	--	--	--	--	4	--	--	--	--	--
Allen	1,119	--	--	--	--	--	--	62	--	278	82	--	--
Bartholomew	295	--	--	--	--	--	--	11	1	--	17	--	--
Blackford	13	--	--	--	--	--	--	4	0	--	--	--	--
Boone	74	--	--	--	--	--	--	26	--	--	1	--	--
Carroll	187	--	--	--	--	--	--	8	--	7	3	--	--
Cass	189	--	--	--	--	--	--	18	--	2	--	--	--
Clinton	54	--	--	--	--	--	--	3	--	--	3	--	--
De Kalb	300	--	--	--	--	--	--	39	--	22	0	--	--
Decatur	310	--	--	--	--	--	--	6	--	--	2	--	--
Delaware	25	--	--	--	--	--	--	1	--	--	--	--	--
Elkhart	443	--	--	7	--	--	7	72	0	7	14	--	--
Fountain	202	--	--	--	--	--	--	15	--	1	0	--	--
Fulton	102	--	--	--	--	--	--	9	--	6	--	--	--
Grant	122	--	--	--	--	--	--	29	0	1	--	--	--
Hamilton	57	--	--	--	--	--	--	16	--	--	--	--	--
Hancock	48	--	--	--	--	--	--	11	--	--	--	--	--
Hendricks	50	--	--	--	--	--	--	10	--	0	--	--	--
Henry	32	--	--	--	--	--	--	1	--	1	--	--	--
Howard	52	--	--	--	--	--	--	9	--	1	10	--	--
Huntington	206	--	--	--	--	--	--	88	0	13	--	--	--
Jasper	83	--	--	--	--	--	--	--	--	--	--	--	--
Jay	176	--	--	--	--	--	--	42	0	2	1	--	--
Johnson	181	--	--	--	--	--	--	63	--	--	7	--	--
Kosciusko	859	--	--	--	--	--	--	223	0	13	7	--	--
La Grange	394	--	--	2	17	--	19	27	2	13	0	--	--
La Porte	205	--	--	--	--	--	--	0	--	--	--	--	--
Lake	40	--	--	--	--	--	--	0	0	--	--	--	--
Madison	50	--	--	--	--	--	--	28	--	2	--	--	--
Marion	56	--	--	--	--	--	--	18	--	0	--	--	--
Marshall	341	--	--	--	--	--	--	18	--	7	1	--	--
Miami	212	--	--	--	--	--	--	41	0	5	0	--	--
Montgomery	159	--	--	--	--	--	--	22	2	1	--	--	--

(Table 13 continued on the next page)

Table 13.—continued

County	(1)	(2)	(3)	(4)	(5)	(6)	(7)	(8)	(9)	(10)	(11)
Newton	48	--	--	--	--	--	--	--	--	--	--
Noble	545	--	--	--	--	--	--	42	--	2	4
Porter	164	--	--	--	--	--	--	2	0	--	--
Pulaski	390	--	--	--	--	--	--	--	--	--	--
Randolph	104	--	--	--	--	--	--	10	--	--	1
Rush	65	--	--	--	--	--	--	21	--	--	--
Shelby	72	--	--	--	--	--	--	13	--	--	--
St. Joseph	459	--	--	--	--	--	--	14	--	--	4
Starke	113	--	--	--	--	--	--	--	--	--	0
Steuben	589	--	--	--	--	--	--	61	1	5	0
Tippecanoe	68	--	--	--	--	--	--	10	--	0	--
Tipton	2	--	--	--	--	--	--	0	--	--	--
Wabash	183	--	--	--	--	1	1	51	--	8	1
Warren	142	--	--	--	--	--	--	5	--	3	--
Wayne	27	--	--	--	--	--	--	3	--	--	--
Wells	144	--	--	--	--	--	--	26	--	0	--
White	113	--	--	--	--	--	--	4	--	4	--
Whitley	372	--	--	10	51	51	51	22	5	14	--
Unit total	**10,329**	--	--	10	68	51	78	1,211	11	420	156
Upland Flats Unit											
Dearborn	308	0	--	--	--	--	--	39	--	2	--
Fayette	181	0	--	--	--	--	--	49	--	--	0
Franklin	457	--	--	--	--	--	--	39	--	--	5
Jefferson	657	9	3	--	3	--	15	31	--	43	3
Jennings	1,203	4	--	--	37	--	--	68	41	13	54
Ohio	49	0	--	--	--	--	--	22	--	--	--
Ripley	672	4	--	--	--	--	--	49	--	18	28
Switzerland	71	4	--	--	--	--	--	12	--	--	--
Union	87	0	--	--	--	--	--	10	--	--	1
Unit total	**3,685**	22	3	10	40	3	65	319	41	76	91
State total	**50,639**	48	44	10	851	651	1,604	3,671	41	579	924

(Additional all-dash / zero columns to the right total 0.)

Forest Inventory Unit and county	Black cherry	Black walnut	Cotton-wood	Elm	Hickory	Hard maple	Soft maple	Red oak group	White oak group	Sweet-gum	Syca-more	Tupelo/gum	Yellow-poplar	Other hardwoods	Total hardwoods
Knobs Unit															
Brown	61	7	--	5	249	167	95	1,031	671	0	2	48	119	43	2,593
Clark	12	11	--	0	89	46	13	121	107	24	--	13	277	8	881
Crawford	42	4	--	3	194	126	12	390	447	--	1	46	178	25	1,505
Dubois	56	17	--	1	106	93	67	211	215	19	1	20	248	85	1,253
Floyd	7	2	--	--	15	29	4	70	158	0	0	--	11	11	344
Harrison	106	9	1	5	70	164	18	288	120	--	1	5	161	41	1,122
Jackson	61	10	7	2	88	195	108	303	270	40	2	125	600	30	2,137
Lawrence	119	16	3	5	103	139	38	503	233	--	1	105	761	65	2,229
Monroe	117	53	--	5	340	156	51	469	522	5	0	22	664	59	2,712
Morgan	15	9	62	1	92	136	49	267	77	--	1	17	330	31	1,291
Orange	36	20	--	3	106	215	18	546	338	7	1	40	596	108	2,145
Owen	6	4	2	2	116	156	39	175	110	2	1	6	743	28	1,544
Perry	15	3	--	4	153	144	42	260	340	9	2	8	142	21	1,192
Scott	11	6	--	0	23	74	4	4	84	1	2	1	95	8	329
Spencer	34	3	--	0	88	22	40	85	67	17	--	17	6	33	479
Warrick	4	2	26	1	54	18	37	228	49	15	1	28	25	16	546
Washington	94	18	--	5	222	268	9	364	592	--	1	36	773	30	2,642
Unit total	795	196	101	44	2,107	2,148	646	5,316	4,400	139	18	539	5,731	643	24,944
Lower Wabash Unit															
Clay	26	8	--	2	37	64	92	284	39	3	--	30	182	9	831
Daviess	13	2	81	1	31	11	76	148	33	6	0	2	134	28	600
Gibson	8	3	21	0	44	13	52	37	1	5	--	12	4	39	291
Greene	76	8	45	1	160	83	139	295	124	2	2	52	848	70	1,943
Knox	0	6	1	0	1	32	8	65	2	1	--	1	126	20	325
Martin	29	4	5	2	264	180	33	305	279	--	5	27	593	23	1,885
Parke	71	28	--	6	91	123	4	190	185	--	--	52	407	86	1,389
P ke	14	1	62	1	17	14	14	74	8	25	1	20	30	38	332
Posey	4	0	--	0	12	2	6	62	22	6	1	3	11	8	157
Putnam	34	32	--	1	214	126	26	126	127	--	1	1	338	42	1,182
Sullivan	24	16	2	2	81	7	16	137	17	--	0	49	65	43	534
Vanderburgh	0	--	44	0	1	8	8	7	0	3	--	1	9	0	85
Vermillion	4	1	--	--	16	2	--	80	14	--	--	0	25	6	154
Vigo	35	11	12	3	38	39	98	111	28	--	--	20	35	35	511
Unit total	338	120	273	21	1,005	699	571	1,921	879	50	9	271	2,806	449	10,220

(Table 13 continued on the next page)

Table 13.—continued

Forest Inventory Unit and county	Black cherry	Black walnut	Cotton-wood	Elm	Hickory	Hard maple	Soft maple	Red oak group	White oak group	Sweet-gum	Syca-more	Tupelo/gum	Yellow-poplar	Other hardwoods	Total hardwoods
Northern Unit															
Adams	10	2	0	1	13	1	--	21	37	4	--	1	1	0	95
Allen	15	28	0	8	61	123	46	190	213	4	--	0	3	6	1,119
Bartholomew	2	1	--	1	15	19	11	82	15	12	--	7	100	1	295
Blackford	0	2	1	0	1	1	0	3	1	--	--	--	--	--	13
Boone	3	1	--	3	6	3	0	6	14	9	--	--	--	1	74
Carroll	7	4	24	--	13	13	29	35	45	--	0	0	0	--	187
Cass	10	2	--	0	7	24	1	75	47	3	--	0	0	--	189
Clinton	--	0	17	--	3	3	3	3	3	--	--	6	9	2	54
De Kalb	9	8	0	9	8	24	88	19	17	4	--	47	6	0	300
Decatur	1	3	0	2	15	7	12	75	54	2	--	26	104	1	310
Delaware	9	1	0	0	1	8	--	1	1	--	--	--	2	2	25
Elkhart	79	14	47	20	31	18	43	32	4	4	--	11	32	8	436
Fountain	21	8	33	3	8	32	16	34	7	--	--	13	7	4	202
Fulton	13	2	--	1	7	7	2	38	11	--	--	--	5	0	102
Grant	2	8	4	0	22	11	1	4	39	--	--	--	2	--	122
Hamilton	5	2	--	1	25	0	--	--	--	--	--	6	1	--	57
Hancock	2	5	--	0	4	13	1	7	3	--	--	--	2	--	48
Hendricks	18	3	10	1	0	--	1	0	--	--	--	--	--	7	50
Henry	4	2	--	0	1	1	0	3	9	--	--	6	4	--	32
Howard	6	2	1	0	2	11	1	8	4	--	--	5	1	--	52
Huntington	6	6	10	1	28	13	8	2	5	--	--	14	2	1	206
Jasper	9	0	--	1	5	--	22	14	33	--	--	--	--	--	83
Jay	1	1	1	0	24	16	17	25	47	--	--	--	--	--	176
Johnson	15	7	--	1	36	17	1	15	5	--	--	7	3	3	181
Kosciusko	39	9	105	16	20	68	80	74	103	9	0	58	14	19	859
La Grange	35	10	26	9	26	28	39	18	51	4	--	24	52	12	375
La Porte	79	4	--	0	2	0	22	73	1	--	--	--	22	0	205
Lake	5	0	--	--	1	--	--	1	32	--	--	--	--	--	40
Madison	6	0	--	0	1	1	2	6	1	--	0	--	2	--	50
Marion	0	2	--	1	3	1	1	0	0	--	--	10	17	1	56
Marshall	54	7	47	2	12	29	42	72	24	5	--	6	10	5	341
Miami	10	11	10	1	2	39	10	41	23	--	0	5	12	1	212
Montgomery	7	19	2	2	18	20	0	22	10	--	--	4	23	7	159

County														Total
Newton	5	0	--	0	--	5	17	20	--	--	--	--	--	48
Noble	78	12	1	22	59	60	76	157	4	--	0	2	17	545
Porter	5	0	51	6	14	6	26	44	0	--	--	7	--	164
Pulaski	3	2	78	2	--	43	131	131	--	--	--	--	--	390
Randolph	2	1	--	7	17	--	15	49	--	--	--	2	0	104
Rush	2	2	3	6	9	2	2	2	--	0	13	3	0	65
Shelby	0	0	32	--	6	1	--	13	--	--	7	--	--	72
St. Joseph	52	2	--	16	8	43	237	40	1	--	5	18	14	459
Starke	1	1	1	4	2	21	58	19	7	--	--	--	--	113
Steuben	36	19	36	32	21	16	90	94	4	--	43	108	10	589
Tippecanoe	0	6	--	12	--	1	29	4	--	--	--	2	3	68
Tipton	--	0	1	--	--	0	--	--	--	--	--	--	0	2
Wabash	13	4	0	11	25	7	48	10	--	--	2	0	1	182
Warren	7	3	--	0	2	--	8	51	--	--	18	43	0	142
Wayne	2	1	--	6	3	0	6	2	--	--	2	2	--	27
Wells	0	6	--	5	9	2	4	87	--	--	3	1	--	144
White	3	1	17	4	0	11	51	17	--	--	--	0	--	113
Whitley	21	7	48	35	78	3	13	29	4	0	13	7	11	321
Unit total	713	242	607	589	804	719	1,811	1,625	78	0	362	632	142	10,251
Upland Flats Unit														
Dearborn	16	7	--	32	11	2	95	88	--	--	6	2	5	307
Fayette	23	2	--	7	11	1	7	15	--	--	13	50	3	181
Franklin	12	4	10	43	18	8	117	79	3	--	29	82	4	457
Jefferson	9	14	--	34	28	44	175	31	63	0	21	143	1	642
Jennings	29	4	0	80	36	48	146	189	30	--	37	424	2	1,162
Ohio	4	0	--	0	2	--	9	4	--	--	--	6	0	49
Ripley	24	4	--	42	68	34	61	111	83	--	36	99	8	668
Switzerland	1	4	--	19	2	5	2	14	--	--	6	1	2	67
Union	20	1	1	24	6	--	4	2	--	--	16	1	1	87
Unit total	137	41	11	280	180	143	618	533	180	0	164	807	27	3,620
State total	1,983	598	992	3,980	3,831	2,078	9,665	7,437	446	27	1,336	9,976	1,261	49,035

All table cells without observations are indicated by -- . Table value of 0 indicates the volume rounds to less than 1 thousand cubic feet. Columns and rows may not add to their totals due to rounding.

Table 14.—Disposition of residues produced at primary wood-using mills, in thousand tons, green weight, by Forest Inventory Unit, disposition, residue type, and softwoods and hardwoods, Indiana, 2008

Forest Inventory Unit and disposition	Total all residues		Total wood residue		Residue type — Wood residue — Coarse		Fine		Bark	
	Softwood	Hardwood	Softwood	Hardwood	Softwood	Hardwood	Softwood	Hardwood	Softwood	Hardwood
All Units										
Fiber products	1.04	289.32	1.04	289.03	1.04	272.75	–	16.28	–	0.29
Industrial fuel	1.08	138.31	1.01	132.43	0.91	73.94	0.10	58.49	0.07	5.88
Domestic fuel	0.46	32.94	0.19	27.29	0.19	26.99	–	0.30	0.27	5.65
Mulch	4.68	328.09	0.83	125.46	0.83	112.49	0.00	12.97	3.85	202.63
Pellets	–	35.21	–	32.68	–	20.82	–	11.85	–	2.53
Miscellaneous[a]	9.13	189.62	9.13	178.79	4.49	40.97	4.64	137.83	0.00	10.83
Not used	0.05	3.60	0.05	2.87	–	1.83	0.05	1.05	–	0.73
State total	16.45	1,017.09	12.25	788.54	7.45	549.78	4.79	238.75	4.20	228.55
Knobs Unit										
Fiber products	1.04	120.57	1.04	120.28	1.04	110.86	–	9.42	–	0.29
Industrial fuel	0.86	45.90	0.81	42.12	0.72	18.87	0.09	23.25	0.05	3.78
Domestic fuel	0.03	9.85	0.02	8.17	0.02	8.17	0.00	–	0.01	1.68
Mulch	4.64	169.76	0.83	86.11	0.83	76.12	0.00	9.99	3.81	83.65
Miscellaneous[a]	8.90	91.09	8.90	83.00	4.49	15.06	4.41	67.94	0.00	8.09
Not used	0.05	0.93	0.05	0.88	–	0.04	0.05	0.84	–	0.05
Unit total	15.52	438.10	11.65	340.56	7.10	229.11	4.55	111.45	3.87	97.54
Lower Wabash Unit										
Fiber products	–	95.58	–	95.58	–	88.72	–	6.85	–	–
Industrial fuel	–	10.35	–	10.35	–	3.93	–	6.42	–	–
Domestic fuel	0.04	3.24	0.03	2.30	0.03	2.30	–	–	0.01	0.94
Mulch	–	54.32	–	8.50	–	5.52	–	2.98	–	45.82
Miscellaneous[a]	0.01	39.26	0.01	38.96	–	12.08	0.01	26.88	–	0.30
Not used	–	0.37	–	0.34	–	0.18	–	0.15	–	0.03
Unit total	0.05	203.12	0.04	156.03	0.03	112.74	0.01	43.29	0.01	47.09
Northern Unit										
Fiber products	–	56.54	–	56.54	–	56.54	–	–	–	–
Industrial fuel	0.15	80.72	0.15	79.00	0.14	50.20	0.01	28.81	0.01	1.72
Domestic fuel	0.39	18.30	0.14	15.64	0.14	15.61	–	0.03	0.25	2.66
Mulch	0.05	98.99	–	30.84	–	30.84	–	–	0.05	68.15
Pellets	–	31.95	–	31.94	–	20.08	–	11.85	–	0.01
Miscellaneous[a]	0.21	46.61	0.21	44.20	–	12.85	0.21	31.35	–	2.41
Not used	–	0.02	–	0.02	–	–	–	0.02	–	–
Unit total	0.80	333.14	0.50	258.19	0.29	186.13	0.22	72.07	0.30	74.95
Upland Flats Unit										
Fiber products	–	16.63	–	16.63	–	16.63	–	–	–	–
Industrial fuel	0.06	1.34	0.04	0.95	0.04	0.95	–	–	0.02	0.39
Domestic fuel	–	1.54	–	1.18	–	0.91	–	0.27	–	0.36
Mulch	–	5.02	–	–	–	–	–	–	–	5.02
Pellets	–	3.26	–	0.74	–	0.74	–	–	–	2.52
Miscellaneous[a]	0.01	12.65	0.01	12.63	–	0.98	0.01	11.66	–	0.02
Not used	–	2.28	–	1.63	–	1.60	–	0.03	–	0.65
Unit total	0.08	42.73	0.06	33.76	0.04	21.81	0.01	11.95	0.02	8.97

[a] Livestock bedding, small dimension, and specialty items.

All table cells without observations are indicated by –. Table value of 0.00 indicates the volume rounds to less than 0.01 thousand green tons. Columns and rows may not add to their totals due to rounding.